FOCUS GROUPS AS QUALITATIVE RESEARCH

DAVID L. MORGAN
Portland State University

Qualitative Research Methods Series
Volume 16
Second Edition

SAGE PUBLICATIONS
International Educational and Professional Publisher
Thousand Oaks   London   New Delhi

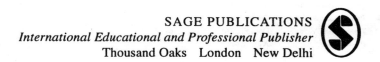

For information address:

SAGE Publications, Inc.
2455 Teller Road
Thousand Oaks, California 91320
E-mail: order@sagepub.com

SAGE Publications Ltd.
6 Bonhill Street
London EC2A 4PU
United Kingdom

SAGE Publications India Pvt. Ltd.
M-32 Market
Greater Kailash I
New Delhi 110 048 India

Printed in the United States of America

Library of Congress Cataloging-in-Publication Data

Morgan, David L.
  Focus groups as qualitative research / David L. Morgan. — 2nd ed.
    p. cm. — (Qualitative research methods ; v. 16)
  Includes bibliographical references and index.
  ISBN 0-7619-0342-9 (alk. paper). — ISBN 0-7619-0343-7 (pbk. :
alk. paper)
    1. Focused group interviewing. 2. Social sciences—Research-
-Methodology. I. Title. II. Series.
  H61.28.M67 1997
  300'.723—dc20   96-25389

    98 99 00 01 02 03 10 9 8 7 6 5 4

Acquiring Editor:	Peter Labella
Editorial Assistant:	Francis Borghi
Production Editor:	Sherrise Purdum
Production Assistant:	Denise Santoyo
Typesetter/Designer:	Danielle Dillahunt
Print Buyer:	Anna Chin

CONTENTS

SERIES EDITORS' INTRODUCTION

Only a decade ago, focus groups were virtually unknown to social scientists. Now, their use in academic settings as well as outside is vast and ever-growing. In this extensively revised and updated edition of *Focus Groups as Qualitative Research,* David Morgan provides an excellent guide to focus groups. He carefully considers their many uses in the research enterprise and discusses effective planning and research design for focus groups. Finally, he provides concrete and practical advice on how to conduct and analyze focus groups and considers additional possibilities.

One of the best-selling titles in the *Qualitative Research Methods* series, this revision will be of value to qualitative researchers in every academic discipline as well as those in nonacademic settings.

John Van Maanen
Peter K. Manning
Marc L. Miller

PREFACE

Much has changed during the 10 years since I began work on the first edition of this book. The most rewarding of these changes is the fact that focus groups are now a much more widely practiced research method within the social sciences. Indeed, this increasing experience with focus groups in the social sciences is the primary reason for this new edition. Ten years ago, nearly all the recent writing on focus groups came from marketing research. Today, there is a sizable literature about focus groups in anthropology, communication studies, education, evaluation, nursing, political science, psychology, public health, sociology, and many other disciplines. Indeed, more than half the references cited in this book were published since the previous edition.

During those 10 years, I too have been busy. In that time, I have conducted more than 20 research projects involving more than 100 focus groups, as well as leading numerous training sessions and workshops. Thinking back over these past few years makes me realize how much I owe to those who were there at the beginning: Pamela G. Smith, who first drew my attention to focus groups, and Margaret Spanish, who both assisted me with and coauthored my first work in this field. Of course, I would never have been prepared to take advantage of those opportunities without the graduate training that I received from Bill Gamson in working with groups and from the late David Street in qualitative methods.

It takes a team of people working together to make a focus group's project succeed. It has taken many more to help focus groups become better known. I have been fortunate to have good company in sharing these tasks. One particularly pleasant aspect of my work on focus groups has been the collaboration that Richard Krueger and I have developed. Although Dick and I had never met when Sage published our two books on focus groups in 1988, we have since had many chances to talk and work together in ways that continue to be enlightening to me. Over the years, I have also benefited from repeated exchanges with my colleagues Robin Jarrett, John Knodel, and Kerth O'Brien, as well as from discussions with many other social scientists who have helped me to pursue my interest in focus groups, including Duane Alwin, Gene Anderson, Janet Mancini Billson, Linda Boise, Edgar Butler, Martha Ann Carey, Ben Crabtree, Ted Fuller, Bill Gamson, Bob Hanneman, John Kennedy, Will Miller, Jan Morse, Eliot Smith, Richard Zeller, and Mary Zinkin. I have been fortunate to work with many talented graduate students, and I especially recognize Paula Carder, Marie Duncan, Steve March, and Alice Scannell for their assistance with multiple projects over the years. In addition, like so many other Sage authors, I owe a special debt to Mitch Allen for all his assistance and insights over the years. Finally, I want to thank my wife, Susan Wladaver-Morgan, not just for her consistently professional editing of my work but also for all the many other ways in which she has supported my work.

FOCUS GROUPS AS QUALITATIVE RESEARCH

DAVID L. MORGAN
Portland State University

1. INTRODUCTION

In a church meeting room, a group of widows compare their experiences. One woman complains that other people wanted her to stop grieving in 6 months, but that it really takes much longer. Another woman produces murmurs of agreement throughout the groups when she adds that the second year is sometimes harder than the first (Morgan, 1989).

In a living room, a group of working people discuss their views of major political topics such as affirmative action, nuclear power, and the Arab-Israeli conflict. One striking element of their conversations is the number of personal connections that they make to these issues, even when they react to examples of how the mass media portray these topics (Gamson, 1992).

In a rural village in Thailand, two groups, one of young men and one of young women, discuss the number of children they want to have and how this has changed since their parents' day. Elsewhere in the same village, groups from the older generation discuss how they feel about this issue and how things have changed for their children. Later, the researcher analyzes tapes of these discussions to compare the thoughts and experiences of men and women in the older and younger generation (Knodel, Havanon, & Pramualratana, 1984).

In Chicago, a group of young African American mothers talk about what it is like to be on welfare. They all agree that it is a hard life, but to hear them tell it they have what it takes to get along despite their obvious problems. Still, as the discussion wears on, their stories are more and more about how hard it is and less about their own ability to rise above their circumstances (Jarrett, 1993).

Each of these examples describes a piece of research using focus groups. As a form of qualitative research, focus groups are basically group interviews, although not in the sense of an alternation between a researcher's questions and the research participants' responses. Instead, the reliance is on interaction within the group, based on topics that are supplied by the researcher who typically takes the role of a moderator. The hallmark of focus groups is their explicit use of group interaction to produce data and insights that would be less accessible without the interaction found in a group.

Only a decade ago, focus groups were almost unknown to social scientists. Now, a review of on-line databases (Morgan, 1996) indicates that research using focus groups is appearing in academic journals at the rate of more than 100 articles per year. Their use in applied research outside academic settings is even more extensive. This rapid growth is partly due to social scientists' ability to borrow from an established set of practices in marketing research, in which focus groups have been the dominant form of qualitative data collection (e.g., Goldman & MacDonald, 1987; Greenbaum, 1993; Hayes & Tatham, 1989). The other major factor driving the growth of focus groups has been social scientists' ability to adapt this technique to our own purposes (e.g., Krueger, 1994; Morgan, 1993a; Stewart & Shamdasani, 1990; Vaughn, Schumm, & Sinagub, 1996). The recent history of focus groups in the social sciences has thus been one of both considerable borrowing and considerable innovation.

Uses for Focus Groups

The on-line search referred to previously revealed three basic uses for focus groups in current social science research. First, they are used as a *self-contained* method in studies in which they serve as the principal source of data. Second, they are used as a *supplementary* source of data in studies that rely on some other primary method such as a survey. Third, they are used in *multimethod* studies that combine two or more means of gathering data in which no one primary method determines the use of the others.

In the self-contained uses, focus groups serve as the primary means of collecting qualitative data, just as participant observation or individual interviewing can serve as a primary means of gathering data. Using focus groups in this manner requires a careful matching of the goals of the research with the data that the focus groups can produce to meet these goals. Accordingly, the use of focus groups as a self-contained method often leads to an emphasis on research design.

In supplementary uses of focus groups, the group discussions often serve as a source of preliminary data in a primarily quantitative study. For example, they can be used to generate survey questionnaires or to develop the content of applied programs and interventions. The focus groups could also serve as a source of follow-up data to assist the primary method. For instance, they might be used to pursue poorly understood survey results or to evaluate the outcome of a program or intervention. In these supplementary uses of focus groups, the groups must be set up and conducted in ways that maximize their value for the primary method.

In multimethod uses, focus groups typically add to the data that are gathered through other qualitative methods, such as participant observation and individual interviews. The model here is clearly ethnography, which has traditionally involved a blend of observation and interviewing. Bringing focus groups into this combination simply means using group as well as individual interviews (e.g., Willis, 1977). In these combined uses of qualitative methods, the goal is to use each method so that it contributes something unique to the researcher's understanding of the phenomenon under study. The relative place of focus groups within this mix of methods would depend on the researcher's data needs, the opportunities and limitations of the field setting, and so on.

Focus groups can thus serve a number of different purposes. Used in a self-contained fashion, they can be the basis for a complete study. Used with other methods, they can either supplement another primary method or combine with other qualitative methods in a true partnership. This flexible range of uses for focus groups in the social sciences contrasts strongly with marketing applications in which focus groups have historically served as a preliminary step to be followed by quantitative research (McQuarrie, 1996). Given the strong tradition of qualitative research in the social sciences, researchers in these fields have understandably taken a broader approach to the uses of focus groups. Even so, the options we have currently developed certainly do not exhaust the possible uses of focus groups, and there are undoubtedly many other creative uses of focus groups still waiting to be discovered.

Focus Groups in Historical Perspective

Focus groups are not really new. Within the social sciences, Bogardus's (1926) description of group interviews is among the earliest published work. Group interviews also played a notable part in applied social research programs during World War II, including efforts to examine the persuasiveness of propaganda efforts and the effectiveness of training materials for the troops (Merton & Kendall, 1946), as well as studies on factors that affected the productivity of work groups (Thompson & Demerath, 1952). It was these wartime efforts that produced the first detailed discussions of group interviews, which evolved from a mimeographed manual to a recently reissued book (Merton, Fiske, & Kendall, 1990). At about the same time, focus groups were transplanted into marketing research by Paul Lazarsfeld and others. Indeed, it was Lazarsfeld, a colleague of Merton's at Columbia, whose program of research on audience response to radio broadcasts first introduced Merton to group interviews (Merton et al., 1990; Rogers, 1994). Although his fellow sociologists have emphasized Lazarsfeld's contributions to quantitative research, marketers have always given equal time to his qualitative work—a balance that was important to Lazarsfeld himself (see Lazarsfeld, 1972), as was his dual involvement in academics and marketing.

Given such auspicious origins, why did focus groups virtually disappear from the social sciences during the next three decades? One likely reason is that Merton et al. (1990) explicitly limited the uses of "focused interviews" to gauging reaction stimulus materials, such as films, radio broadcasts, and written manuals. Furthermore, neither Merton nor his colleagues published much research that used group interviews. For example, *The Student Physician* (Merton, Reader, & Kendall, 1957) made extensive use of tabulations from survey data and quoted liberally from diaries that the students kept, but the authors made only passing mention of the fact that they also used group interviews. During this same time, work with groups became closely associated with small group decision making in social psychology, whereas most of the development of qualitative methods centered on participant observation and individual interviewing (Becker & Greer, 1957). The basic reason that focus groups did not take hold earlier thus appears to be neglect, both by the technique's original proponents, who turned to other pursuits, and by its potential users, who concentrated on other methods.

Even so, various versions of the group interview have been a frequent, if incidental, feature of qualitative research. Examples would include

Irwin's (1970) interviews with groups of prisoners in *The Felon*, Hochschild's (1983) group interviews with stewardesses in *The Managed Heart*, or Gubrium's (1987) observations of a support group in *Old Timers and Alzheimer's*. In most of these cases, group interviews were used primarily for convenience—either groups allowed more individuals to be reached at once or groups were where the participants were most likely to be located. Perhaps because of this emphasis on simple convenience, group interviewing was not systematically developed as a research technique in the social sciences until recently.

In the early 1980s, applied demographers (e.g., Folch-Lyon, de la Macorra, & Schearer, 1981) began to use focus groups as a way to understand the knowledge, attitudes, and practices that influenced the use of contraception. At about the same time, British communication researchers began using focus groups to examine how audience members interpreted media messages (Lunt & Livingstone, 1996). With the advent of the acquired immunodeficiency syndrome epidemic, researchers (e.g., Joseph et al., 1984) used focus groups as a first step to overcome their limited knowledge about the gay community. Meanwhile, other health educators (e.g., Basch, 1987) were improving the effectiveness of intervention programs by holding group discussions with members of their target audience. Oral history provided other applications (Ingersoll & Ingersoll, 1987). A landmark occurred in 1987 with the first publication of book-length texts on focus groups by marketers, several of which are now in second editions (Goldman & McDonald, 1987; Greenbaum, 1993; Templeton, 1994). The social sciences were not far behind. In 1988, the first edition of this book appeared along with the first edition of Krueger's text (1994), which fueled the interest in focus groups as a tool in evaluation research. Given the existence of these resources, as well as subsequent books (Stewart & Shamdasani, 1990; Vaughn et al., 1996) and special issues of journals (Carey, 1995; Knodel, 1995), focus groups have become an increasingly well-known method for collecting qualitative data.

Focus Groups and Group Interviews

One question that has accompanied the rising use of group interviews has been whether the label "focus groups" fits all these different applications. According to one school of thought (Frey & Fontana, 1989; Khan & Manderson, 1992), we need to develop a typology of different kinds of group interviews, which would define focus groups as one specific form of group interview. The "exclusive approach" emphasizes the need to determine which forms of group interview are or are not focus groups. My own preference (Morgan, 1996) is for a more inclusive approach that broadly defines focus groups as a research technique that collects data through group interaction on a topic determined by the researcher. In essence, it is the researcher's interest that provides the focus, whereas the data themselves come from the group interaction.

One reason for favoring an inclusive approach is that the exclusive approaches do not really exclude very much. Other than focus groups, the primary categories of group interviews in the existing typologies are things that are manifestly different from focus groups. On the one hand, there are nominal groups and Delphi groups (Stewart & Shamdasani, 1990), which do not involve actual group interaction. On the other hand, there is the observation of naturally occurring groups, which typically do not involve the researcher in determining the topic of discussion. Thus, little is gained by excluding these categories of data collection because they already fall outside the broad definition of focus groups offered here.

Among the more specific criteria that could be used to distinguish focus groups from other types of group interviews, both Frey and Fontana (1989) and Khan and Manderson (1992) assert that focus groups are more formal. In particular, they argue that focus groups are likely to involve inviting participants to the discussion and they also stress the distinctive role of the moderator. Although there is no doubt that group interviews vary along a continuum from more formally structured interaction to more informal gatherings, I do not believe it is possible to draw a line between formal and informal group interviews in a way that defines some as focus groups and others as something else. Instead, I find it more useful to think that the degree of formal structure in a focus group is a decision that the research makes according to the specific purposes of the research project. In particular, the use of either a more formal or a less formal approach will depend on the researcher's goals, the nature of the research setting, and the likely reaction of the participants to the research topic.

Among the other criteria that have been offered as distinguishing features of focus groups are their size and the use of specialized facilities for the interview (McQuarrie, 1996). Again, however, these supposedly exclusive criteria are mostly a matter of degree. Who is to say when a group is too large or too small to be called a focus group or when a setting is too casual to qualify? Rather than generate pointless debates about what is or is not a focus group, I prefer to treat focus groups as a "broad umbrella" or "big tent" that can include many different variations. Of course, this approach requires researchers to make choices about doing focus groups one way rather than another. Fortunately, this need to make explicit decisions about data collection strategies is a familiar concern to social scientists, and it comes under the heading of "research design." As social scientists have gained increasing experience with focus groups, we also have produced insights into the situations in which different research designs are either more or less likely to be effective (e.g., Krueger, 1993; Morgan, 1992a, 1995).

Overview of the Remainder of This Book

The ultimate goal of this book is to provide the motivated reader with the wherewithal to conduct effective focus group research. Although a slim volume such as this cannot produce "instant experts," it can provide a basis for growth in an area that resembles many things we already do. Much of what goes into conducting focus groups touches on the same issues that arise in any effort to collect qualitative data. Thus, a continuing theme of this book is that those of us who become focus group researchers are simply occupying a natural niche within the well-defined territory of qualitative research methodology.

The next chapter compares focus groups to the two most common means of gathering qualitative data—individual interviewing and participant observation—and uses this comparison to locate the strengths and weaknesses of focus groups. Chapter 3 presents a variety of different applications for focus groups as a research technique, both as a self-contained means of collecting data and in combination with other methods. Chapter 4 covers the technical aspects involved in planning and designing focus groups. That chapter and the next provide a thorough treatment of the practical issues involved in focus groups, and Chapter 5 presents the fundamental options in conducting focus groups. Chapter 6 examines a variety of additional possibilities that go beyond the basic format. The concluding chapter returns to the theme of focus groups as a qualitative method to look at the potential contributions of this new method to social science research.

2. FOCUS GROUPS AS A QUALITATIVE METHOD

At present, the two principal means of collecting qualitative data in the social sciences are participant observation, which typically occurs in groups, and open-ended interviews, which typically occur with individuals.

As group interviews, focus groups not only occupy an intermediate position between these other qualitative methods but also possess a distinctive identity of their own. On the one hand, focus groups cannot really substitute for the kinds of research that are already done well by either individual interviews or participant observation. On the other hand, focus groups provide access to forms of data that are not obtained easily with either of the other two methods. In this context, it becomes particularly important to understand the strengths and weaknesses of focus groups and to do so in comparison to other qualitative methods. This chapter will first compare focus groups to participant observation and individual interviews and then present an overview of the strengths and weaknesses of focus groups as a qualitative method.

Compared to Participant Observation

The main advantage of focus groups in comparison to participant observation is the opportunity to observe a large amount of interaction on a topic in a limited period of time based on the researcher's ability to assemble and direct the focus group sessions. This control is also a disadvantage, however, because it means that focus groups are in some sense unnatural social settings. Like Gamson (1992), I feel that any intrusion of human observers in a research setting means that we can only talk about the degree to which we are observing a naturalistic setting. Still, my sense is that the degree of naturalism in most participant observation studies is higher than the degree of naturalism in most focus group studies.

What are the actual advantages to observing interaction in naturalistic settings? Three major advantages of naturalistic observation are (a) an ability to collect data on a larger range of behaviors, (b) a greater variety of interactions with the study participants, and (c) a more open discussion of the research topic. By comparison, focus groups are (a) limited to verbal behavior, (b) consist only of interaction in discussion groups, and (c) are created and managed by the researcher.

First, like all forms of interviews, focus groups are largely limited to verbal behavior and self-reported data. If the goal is to collect data on other social actions, rather than just the discussion of these activities, then the increased naturalism of participant observation is necessary. Second, even if focus groups do bring group interaction into the picture, there are still many interactions that cannot be re-created in focus groups. If the interaction of interest does not consist of a "discussion," then more naturalistic observation is probably preferable. Finally, because the discussions in focus groups are controlled by the researcher, we can never be sure of how natural the interactions are. If the topic of interest demands relatively uncontaminated statements of the research participants' experiences and perspectives, then participant observation is the closest approximation to this degree of naturalness.

Although the great strength of participant observation, in comparison to focus groups, consists of more naturalistic observations, its comparative weakness is the difficulty in locating and gaining access to settings in which a substantial set of observations can be collected on the topic of interest. A good example is the research that I did with Margaret Spanish on perceptions of heart attack risk factors (Morgan & Spanish, 1985). What we had in mind was a group of people gathered around a lunch table discussing their surprise over a mutual friend's heart attack, an image that we labeled "Oh my God, not Harry!" Certainly, such interaction occurs, but where could we find the opportunity to observe it? By conducting focus groups, we admittedly had to sacrifice the immediacy and emotion of a naturally occurring episode such as the lunch conversation, but this was not really a loss because we could not "sacrifice" what we never had access to in the first place.

There is a more subtle implication to the value of focus groups in research areas in which a dense set of observations is difficult to locate: We tend to do participant observation in settings in which there is something immediately available to observe. For example, it is easily feasible to do participant observation studies about patients recovering from heart attacks using doctors and hospitals as a point of access. One reason that topics such as social roles and formal organizations are so frequently studied by participant observation is that they are structurally well suited to the method. Of course, the fundamental importance of roles and organizations to social theory is also a factor. More social psychological topics such as attitudes and decision making, however, appear to be slighted in participant observation not because they are less important but because they are less well suited to observation.

Because both focus groups and participant observation share an overlapping interest in group interaction, there are many topics where it would be possible to design a study using either of them. In this case, there is a trade-off—between the naturalness of observations in a field setting and the ability to collect a concentrated set of interactions in a very short span of time via focus groups. This is not the kind of choice that can be made on strictly technical grounds. The different value attached to the advantages and disadvantages of the two methods will depend on the research topic itself, the background and interests of the researcher, and the nature of the ultimate audience for the research. Put simply, where there is a premium on the naturalistic ability to observe group behavior and where the opportunity to observe such behavior is readily available, some form of participant observation will be preferred over focus groups.

Taken together, these various comparisons suggest division of labor between participant observation and focus groups. Participant observation will always have an advantage when it is necessary to observe behaviors in their natural context, and especially when it is necessary to follow these behaviors in-depth over time. Thus, for purposes such as ethnography, focus groups may play a supplementary role, but they certainly will not supplant participant observation as the primary tool for the investigation of broad aspects of culture. There are many other situations, however, in which full-scale participant observation study would be either impractical or inefficient. With regard to practicality, some processes, such as attitude formation and decision making, are inherently unobservable, and some kinds of behaviors are either too private or habit-ridden to offer much opportunity for meaningful observation. With regard to efficiency, there are many topics in which the effort required by participant observation would be excessive or in which here the need for rapid data gathering would supersede the need for the depth and detail of participant observation. In each of these cases, focus groups could well be the preferred method.

Compared to Individual Interviews

The comparative advantage of focus groups as an interview technique lies in their ability to observe interaction on a topic. Group discussions provide direct evidence about similarities and differences in the participants' opinions and experiences as opposed to reaching such conclusions from post hoc analyses of separate statements from each interviewee. This reliance on group interaction, however, also means that individual interviews have clear advantages over focus groups with regard to (a) the amount of control that the interviewer has and (b) the greater amount of information that each informant has time to share. By comparison, focus groups (a) require greater attention to the role of the moderator and (b) provide less depth and detail about the opinions and experiences of any given participant.

The advantages that individual interviews offer in terms of control stem from closer communication between interviewer and informant. Interviewers can thus typically use more subtle cues to control the direction of one-on-one conversations compared to what is necessary to guide a group discussion. Furthermore, Agar and MacDonald (1995) argue that the dynamics of individual interviews put more burden on the informants to explain themselves to the interviewer so that the elaboration of initial statements often occurs with relatively little input from the interviewer. By comparison, focus groups may confront the researcher with a choice between either giving control to the group and possibly hearing less about the topic of interest or taking direct control over the group, and possibly loosing the free-flowing discussion that was the original intent of the group interview.

Issues of control over the interview, however, can sometimes favor focus groups. In particular, group discussions make it easier to conduct "less structured interviews" (see Chapter 4) in which there is no preconstructed interview guideline or questionnaire. This ability to give the group control over the direction of the interview is especially useful in exploratory research in which the researcher may not initially even know what questions to ask. Although individual interviews can be adapted to let participants determine the direction of the interview (e.g., Spradley, 1979), the ability to turn the interaction in the interview over to the participants themselves provides focus groups with a particular strength in this regard.

The other distinct advantage of individual interviews occurs when the goal of the research is to gain an in-depth understanding of a person's opinions and experiences. A 90-minute focus group discussion among 8 to 10 participants will, of necessity, generate roughly a tenth of the information that each participant would provide in an equivalently long individual interview. Therefore, when the goal is to learn about each informant in detail, the individual interview has an obvious advantage. Similarly, when the goal is to learn about the biographical details of a person's life, this argues for the continuity and completeness of the narrative that individual interviews produce.

Interestingly, issues of depth can sometimes favor focus groups. In particular, the individual interview's ability to produce greater depth and continuity is based on an assumption that the informant in fact has more to say. Interestingly, focus groups may have an advantage for topics that are either habit-ridden or not thought out in detail. For example, I once watched a marketer with a background in sociology conduct a lively demonstration focus group of professors and graduate students who discussed their use of bar soap. As an individual interview topic, it would require considerable skill to get an informant to talk about this topic for any length such as an hour. A more relevant example of this principle comes from my research on heart attacks (Morgan & Spanish, 1985). We explicitly sought out age groups that would not have thought very much about what causes or prevents heart attacks. The participants' discussions, however, quickly revealed that they had a range of different thoughts about this topic, which led to a very productive discussion about their agreements and disagreements.

In comparing focus groups and individual interviews, a crucial question is whether the two methods produce similar data. Unfortunately, this topic has been the subject of more speculation (e.g., Agar & MacDonald, 1995) than systematic research. Merton et al. (1990) proposed a useful research design for addressing this issue by interviewing people with both methods, with one half of the sample talking about the topic first in group interviews and then individually and the other half starting with individual interviews. Wight (1994) appears to be the only researcher who has actually followed such a design—in a study of how adolescent males talked about their relations with the opposite sex. He found that when the young men began with focus groups, they voiced a set of boisterous and "macho" claims that they continued to express in subsequent individual interviews. In contrast, a second set of young men who participated in the individual interviews first tended to present themselves as more sensitive to the women's point of view, but this supposed sensitivity disappeared when these youths participated in subsequent group interviews. In other words, three of the four combinations produced a macho response, with the "sensitive" response only appearing in initial individual interviews.

The possibility that individual and group interviews will produce different results immediately raises issues of validity: If the two methods produce different results, then one of them must be wrong. Is this really so? Consider Wight's (1994) results: It seems quite likely that adolescent males will express rather different thoughts about the opposite sex in private than among a group of their peers. In particular, young men may well be capable of both more sensitive and more macho approaches, depending on the context. In reviewing Wight's work, as well as related data of her own, Kitzinger (1994a, 1994b) reached the conclusion that such comparisons of individual and group interviews may be as much about context as validity. Thus, if people actually do act differently in groups than they do alone or in dyads, then group and individual interviews will necessarily demonstrate rather different aspects of the overall behavior pattern.

One answer to this dilemma is to note that an interest in individual behavior might not be well served by data from group interviews. Similarly, a research interest in group behavior might not be well served by data from individual interviews. Most research, however, does not involve topics that can be neatly divided into purely individual or purely group behavior. Therefore, we need to know more about the differences in the content of interviews that may arise from conducting them in dyadic versus group contexts. Sadly, with only one or two studies that provide thorough comparisons of individual and group interviews, it is hard to say much about when such differences in context might lead to differences in results—let alone what the exact nature of those differences might be. Because the question of which method is preferable in which circumstances is essentially an empirical one, it will take more research using both techniques to provide an answer. Only then will we be able to provide useful advice about the topic of the research that might influence the choice of individual interviews or focus groups. With that additional knowledge, we should be better able to make choices about when to use either individual or group interviews or a judicious combination of the two (see Chapter 3).

Strengths and Weaknesses

Pulling together the various strands from these discussions reveals a pattern of strengths and weaknesses for focus groups as a technique for collecting qualitative data. Focus groups are no different from any other method, qualitative or quantitative, in this regard—there are some cases in which they will be preferred and others in which they should be avoided. This summary will argue that both the strengths and the weaknesses of focus groups flow directly from their two defining features: the reliance on the researcher's focus and the group's interaction.

The strength of relying on the researcher's focus is the ability to produce concentrated amounts of data on precisely the topic of interest. This strength was clear in comparison to participant observation because focus groups not only give access to reports on a wide range of topics that may not be observable but also ensure that the data will be directly targeted to the researcher's interests. This strength is one source of focus groups' reputation for being "quick and easy." The other source of this reputation is their relative efficiency in comparison to individual interviews, at least in terms of gathering equivalent amounts of data.

Some accounts of focus groups' ability to gather data efficiently make it sound as if they have an almost magical "synergy" that makes them superior to individual interviews. My own preference is to be much more explicit about the aspects of group interaction that can provide insights into participants' opinions and experiences (see Chapter 3; Morgan, 1996;

Morgan & Krueger, 1993; Morgan & Spanish, 1984). Furthermore, the one study (Fern, 1982) that has used a controlled experiment to compare individual interviews and focus groups showed that group interviews did not produce significantly more or better ideas than an equivalent number of individual interviews. As Fern notes, however, other claims about the supposed superiority of group interaction for purposes other than "idea generation" remain untested—and some are so vague as to be untestable.

A more concrete demonstration of the strength that focus groups offer through concentrated observations on the researcher's interests is the conclusion that two eight-person focus groups would produce as many ideas as 10 individual interviews (Fern, 1982). Given the amount of time that it would take not only to conduct 10 interviews but also to analyze them, working with two focus groups would clearly be more efficient. That does not mean, however, that focus group projects are uniformly easier to accomplish than gathering the equivalent amount of data with individual interviews. Crabtree, Yanoshik, Miller, and O'Connor (1993) point out that logistical factors are often the critical consideration. For example, it may not be practical for some participants to travel to a focus group, or it may be very difficult to assemble enough of the right people for a group. Therefore, there are a number of circumstances in which the logistics would make it more efficient to do individual rather than group interviews.

The fact that focus groups are driven by the researcher's interests can also be a source of weakness, however. The fact that the researcher creates and directs the groups makes them distinctly less naturalistic than participant observation so there is always some residual uncertainty about the accuracy of what the participants say. In particular, there is a very real concern that the moderator, in the name of maintaining the interview's focus, will influence the group's interactions. This problem is hardly unique to focus groups because the researcher influences all but the most unobtrusive social science methods. In reality, there is no hard evidence that the focus group moderator's impact on the data is any greater than the researcher's impact in participant observation or individual interviewing. Indeed, the dyadic nature of individual interviewing would seem to create at least as many opportunities for researcher influence. My own sense is that what makes the issue of the researcher's influence on the data so prominent in focus groups is the moderator's heightened visibility in conducting the interview as opposed to the tendency to remove the interviewer from many accounts of individual interviewing. The researcher's influence on the data, however, is an issue in almost all qualitative research, and those who rely on focus groups must attend to it because it does affect the quality of the data. Even if the concern about the influence of focus group moderators is unreasonably magnified, it is one of those perceptions that can be "real in its consequences"; therefore, focus group researchers must be prepared to respond to this potential criticism.

The second broad source of strength for focus groups is their reliance on interaction in the group to produce the data. As Morgan and Krueger (1993) note, the comparisons that participants make among each other's experiences and opinions are a valuable source of insights into complex behaviors and motivations. Furthermore, in an era when issues of consensus and diversity are of intense interest to social scientists, the discussions in focus groups can provide direct data on these exact issues.

This too produces a corresponding weakness, however, because the group itself may influence the nature of the data it produces. The question of how interacting in a group influences what each individual will contribute to the group is a classic issue in social psychology (e.g., Janis, 1982). The concerns for focus groups include both a tendency toward conformity, in which some participants withhold things that they might say in private, and a tendency toward "polarization," in which some participants express more extreme views in a group than in private (Sussman, Burton, Dent, Stacy, & Flay, 1991). As noted previously, the differences between dyadic interviews versus moderated group discussions is an area that requires much more exploration. It is clear, however, that for some types of participants discussing some types of topics, the presence of a group will affect what they say and how they say it. This is an inevitable aspect of focus groups that should be considered as a potential source of weakness for any given research project.

The group's influence on the discussion can also raise questions about the ability of any particular set of participants to discuss a particular topic. One set of problems involves topics in which the participants' level of involvement is either too low or too high. If the participants have little involvement with a topic, the researcher may collect only scattered instances of the desired material, but if the participants are highly involved with the topic the moderator may have to work hard to control the discussion. A related set of problems arise if the topic is highly controversial or if there is a real potential for disagreement among the participants. This should not, however, leave the impression that topics for focus groups are limited to bland discussions about common topics. In fact, focus groups are routinely used to discuss issues such as family planning (e.g., Knodel et al. 1984) and sexually transmitted diseases (O'Brien, 1993). One simple way to determine whether a topic will work in a focus group setting is to pretest. In this case, the "tone" of the group discussions provides clues about the appropriateness of focus groups. Fortunately, social scientists have taken on the task of investigating the issues involved in working with sensitive topics, especially when cultural differences may be important (e.g., Jarrett, 1993). We have much to learn, however, about the range of practical topics for focus groups, and only further experience will provide better insights into this issue.

Summarizing the strengths of focus groups, we find that what they do best is produce an opportunity to collect data from groups discussing topics of interest to the researcher. This combination of strengths is notably different from the strengths of either participant observation or individual interviews. Because the researcher defines the discussion topics, focus groups are more controlled than participation observation, and because of the participant-defined nature of group interaction the focus group setting is less controlled than individual interviewing. Morgan and Spanish (1984) noted that this compromise between the comparative strengths and weaknesses of the other two techniques bears a resemblance to Howard Becker's (1958) two dimensions for classifying qualitative data. On the first dimension, Becker distinguishes between data that are volunteered by informants and data that are requested by the researcher. The second dimension distinguishes whether the data are publicly presented in the presence of other informants or shared with the researcher alone. The naturalistic advantage of participant observation is that it produces volunteered information in groups, whereas individual interviews emphasize the control available through private contact between the researcher and the participant.

In the case of focus groups, the typical presence of the researcher as a moderator in a focused discussion of a preselected topic means that the data lean toward the researcher-directed and publicly stated poles of the continuum. Focus groups thus offer something of a compromise between the strengths of participant observation and individual interviewing. As a compromise between the strengths and weaknesses of these other two qualitative techniques, focus groups are not as strong as either of them is within their specialized domain. The respective weaknesses of participant observation and individual interviewing, however, allow focus groups to operate across traditional boundaries. This flexibility may be the greatest strength of focus groups. None of this, however, is meant to overstate the strengths of focus groups and, given their potential weaknesses, there are many cases in which focus groups would not be the preferred method.

Summing Up

The issues raised in this chapter really respond to two separate questions. First, when are focus groups a workable alternative for a given research project? Second, given that they are at least possible, when are they actually to be preferred over other qualitative methods?

The simplest test of whether focus groups are appropriate for a research project is to ask how actively and easily the participants would discuss the topic of interest. If there are barriers to active and easy interaction, this may be overcome by some of the discussion techniques described in later chapters. In such a case, it would be wise to build backup data collection strategies into the research design. If researchers use focus groups and are disappointed by the results, however, then it is vital that they find a forum for saying so. At this point, the field of social science focus groups cannot grow without a few public accounts of cases in which focus groups were tried and found inappropriate (e.g., Agar & MacDonald, 1995).

Saying that focus groups are a workable option for a research project is not at all the same as saying that they are the preferred way to gather the data for that project. One goal of this chapter has been the forthright recognition that there are many circumstances in which a different form of qualitative research will produce data that are more appropriate to the researcher's goals. In the same spirit, I have also claimed that there are other circumstances in which focus groups would in fact be preferable to either participant observation or individual interviews. The most basic implication of this argument is that focus groups expand our options when it comes to matching our research questions to qualitative methods.

3. THE USES OF FOCUS GROUPS

This chapter will present focus groups as both a self-contained research method and a technique that can be used in conjunction with other methods. As a self-contained method, focus groups can either explore new research areas or examine well-known research questions from the research participants' own perspective. In combination with other methods, focus groups can provide preliminary research on specific issues in a larger project or follow up research to clarify findings from another method.

Although qualitative researchers in the social sciences have little difficulty with the idea that focus groups can be used as a self-contained means of data collection, there is in fact a long tradition of treating focus groups solely as preliminary or exploratory research that must be backed up by other methods. This is especially true in marketing research (e.g., Greenbaum, 1993; McQuarrie, 1996). In my opinion, this practice is due to the specific purposes that marketers pursue. In particular, when one's goal is sales, then it is vitally important to be able to generalize one's results to target markets. Focus groups by themselves certainly are not adequate for that purpose, and marketers are thus well justified in limiting their use of focus groups as a preliminary or exploratory technique—for their specific needs.

Where the danger arises is in the unwarranted assumption that focus groups must be limited to preliminary or exploratory uses in combination with other methods. For many purposes, focus groups, like other qualitative methods, can be a well-chosen, self-contained means for collecting research data. As researchers, we are often more interested in understanding the particular than the general. Also, we are often more interested in issues of meaning than in precise numerical descriptions. For these and other purposes, focus groups can be used both to generate and to answer research questions.

Self-Contained Focus Groups

The key distinguishing feature of a self-contained focus group is that the results of the research can stand on their own. To give a flavor for this kind of research, I will briefly summarize the four studies that I used to introduce the first chapter.

My own work on widowhood (Morgan, 1989) provides one example of self-contained focus groups. This work was originally inspired by survey researchers' unexpected finding that social support did little to improve the well-being of recent widows. To find out why this might be so, I held a half dozen focus groups primarily with older women who had been widowed in the preceding 6 months to 3 years. Some of these groups were held as special meetings of ongoing widowhood support groups; others consisted of groups that I specifically recruited. In each group, I asked just one question: "What kinds of things have made being widowed either easier for you or harder for you?" Given their intensely shared interest in this topic, these participants were easily able to discuss it for over 2 hours with only minimal guidance from me. They made it abundantly clear that the actions of others were an important part of what made their experience of widowhood both easier and harder because their discussions were as much about problems and conflicts as they were about social support. I thus concluded that the earlier survey work on social support had taken an overly narrow view of how close relationships affect the adjustment to widowhood.

One of the key distinguishing features of my study on recent widows was the relatively informal or "unstructured" approach that I used in my interviews. I will discuss this aspect of focus groups in more detail in the following two chapters, but for now I want to consider a different example of the ways that self-contained focus groups can be done in more informal ways. William Gamson (1992) conducted a series of "peer group conversations" to hear what working people thought about current political topics by bringing together small groups of acquaintances who met in the living room of one of their members. The researchers first led discussions of such topics as the Arab-Israeli conflict, nuclear power, and affirmative action by asking "When you think about this issue, what comes to mind?" They then showed a set of political cartoons to explore the participants' reactions to these popularized expressions of different views on each issue. In a related piece of research, Sasson (1995) used a similar approach to bring members of neighborhood "crime watch" groups together in their living rooms to discuss their thoughts on various theories about what causes crime. In both these cases, the actual conduct of the interviews was relatively formal, but holding the groups among acquaintances in their own homes contributed to a more informal atmosphere in the discussions themselves.

A different approach to taking focus groups to where the participants live is exemplified by John Knodel and coworkers in Thailand (Knodel, 1993; Knodel, et al., 1984; Pramualratana, Havanon, & Knodel, 1985). They conducted a series of discussions in villages in different regions to learn about the remarkable drop in average family size that had occurred in rural Thailand during the previous decade. As might be imagined, these groups were held in the usual places where villagers themselves met rather than in university seminar rooms or in formal focus group facilities with one-way mirrors. In each village, Knodel et al. worked with four separate groups of men and women who were from either the older generation, who had larger families, or the younger generation, who had smaller ones. Comparisons across these groups led to the conclusion that both men and women from each age group not only attributed the differences in family size to the same basic sources but also felt that smaller families were an appropriate response to the large-scale social changes that were transforming life in rural Thailand.

Questions of cultural differences have also been a frequent topic in self-contained focus groups, and one of their strengths is certainly the fact that they can "give voice" to groups that would not otherwise be heard. Robin Jarrett's (1993, 1994) work among low-income, African American, single mothers is a good example of how focus groups can help us hear the voices of socially marginalized groups. In conducting discussions among these women, Jarrett often heard conversations that began with a degree of assertiveness about how well the participants were doing and how successful they were in avoiding the problems that stereotypically should have defined their lives. As the discussions continued, however, these "idealized accounts" of their lives gave way to detailed examples of the very real hardships they faced and much franker comparisons of the difficulties they each had experienced in coping with poverty.

One common summary of the goal in self-contained focus groups is to learn about participants' attitudes and opinions on the researcher's topic of interest, and these studies clearly illustrate the value of such data. I, however, prefer to go beyond attitudes and opinions to emphasize learning about participants' experiences and perspectives. I emphasize experiences because even self-reported behavior is more useful as data than opinions that have an unknown basis in behavior. I also prefer experiences because a discussion of them produces a livelier group dynamic—people are more than happy to compare their different experiences, whereas they might be reluctant to challenge someone else's opinion. I emphasize perspectives because, although attitudes and opinions are typically treated as small, discrete parts of a participant's thinking, a perspective implies a broader basis for specific attitudes and opinions. An emphasis on perspectives brings together attitudes, opinions, and experiences in an effort to find out not only what participants think about an issue but also how they think about it and why they think the way they do.

The basic argument in favor of self-contained focus groups is that they reveal aspects of experiences and perspectives that would be not as accessible without group interaction. The most obvious result that is observable through interaction (Morgan, 1986; Morgan & Spanish, 1984, 1985) is the way that participants respond to each other: providing agreement and disagreement, asking questions and giving answers, and so on. Consequently, the participants in focus groups often say the most interesting aspect of their discussions is the chance to "share and compare" their ideas and experiences. From the researcher's point of view, this process of sharing and comparing provides the rare opportunity to collect direct evidence on how the participants themselves understand their similarities and differences. This actual observation of consensus and diversity is something that can happen quite powerfully through group interaction.

In focus group discussions, this process of sharing and comparing often has a "Yes, but . . ." quality to it. For example, two people who seem outwardly similar may discover that they have very different perspectives on a particular issue. Conversely, two people who seem to come from very different walks of life may find that they have many experiences in common. Participants often signal such comparisons when they begin their response to another's remarks with a comment such as "I understand what you're saying, but what matters more to me is" or "You know, some of those same things have happened to me" or "I guess my situation is a little different." As Agar (1986) has pointed out, this search for connections among different experiences and perceptions is also what researchers do in trying to understand their data. The process of sharing and comparing among participants is thus one of the most valuable aspects of self-contained focus groups.

Before turning to research designs that combine focus groups with other methods, it is worth considering one final aspect of self-contained focus groups. Although each of the examples in this section relied on focus groups as the primary source of data, many of these studies also used additional methods. One common way that self-contained focus groups go together with other sources of data is as part of a single author's ongoing research program. For example, although Knodel and coworkers reported some parts of their work as self-contained focus groups (e.g., Knodel et al., 1984), they also used other parts in conjunction with analyses of census data on changing fertility patterns in Thailand (e.g., Knodel, Chamratrithirong, & Debavalya, 1987). Another way that self-contained focus groups get paired with other kinds of data is in comparing the results of different studies within the same subfield. For example, my work on recent widowhood (Morgan, 1989) used a set of self-contained focus groups to investigate previous survey research findings. This research not only produced data that could stand alone as a qualitative summary of these widows' experiences but also generated hypotheses that could be tested with further survey data.

The key defining feature of self-contained focus groups is thus not the absence of other methods but rather the ability to report the data from the focus groups as a sufficient body of knowledge. In fact, the ability to make larger connections between the results from very different methods is often highly desirable (Bryman, 1988). Such larger connections across methods should not be confused, however, with the kind of multimethod combinations in which one method plays a subsidiary role to another that is the primary source of data. This latter approach to combining focus groups with other methods is the subject of the remainder of this chapter.

Linking Focus Groups and Individual Interviewing

Chapter 2 both noted the points of contact between individual and group interviewing and put forth the broad argument for combining the two within research projects as a way to explore the most effective uses for each method. This section will continue that earlier exploration of their mutual relevance based on the recognition that these are both interview methods. This discussion will thus emphasize the ways that either focus groups or individual interviews can enhance projects that are based primarily on the other method.

The single most important way that either individual or group interviews can contribute to a project built around the other method is in devising the interview schedule. For instance, preliminary focus groups can provide a useful starting point for individual interviews that involve unfamiliar topics or informants. The basic idea is to use one or two exploratory focus groups to reveal the range of the future informants' thoughts and experiences prior to the first individual interview. Alternatively, preliminary individual interviews can help generate focus group discussion guides by giving a feel for how people think and talk about the topics that the groups will discuss. For example, I conducted relatively unstructured interviews with individual informants prior to conducting focus groups about how family caregivers for people with Alzheimer's disease made the decision to seek a medical diagnosis (Morgan, 1992b). Hearing about these individual informants' experiences in detail provided a basis for asking questions that allowed the group participants to share the full range of their experiences.

A different "supplementary" use for either type of interview would be to learn about differences among potential interviewees. Thus, in an individual-interview project that involved a choice among several sites or population groups, a preliminary round of focus groups would provide a basis for selecting the next set of interviews. This would be especially useful if one set of individual interviews as already completed and the goal was to select among several groups for a comparison to the existing data. Alternatively, when deciding whether to mix certain population segments in focus groups or to listen to them in separate groups, a small number of preliminary individual interviews could show whether the various participants' ways of speaking about the topic would allow for a comfortable conversation. For example, preliminary individual interviews could indicate whether different cultural groups shared not just similar experiences and perspectives but also compatible ways of expressing and interacting around these experiences and perspectives.

A final way to combine focus groups with individual interviews is to conduct one as a follow-up to the other. Following individual interviews with focus groups allows the researcher to explore issues that came up only during the analysis of the interviews. For example, if there appear to be differences in perspective across different categories of informants, then focus groups can help confirm this. Alternatively, follow-up individual interviews can help provide depth and detail on topics that were only broadly discussed in group interviews. For example, in another study of Alzheimer's caregivers (Duncan & Morgan, 1994), we conducted individual, follow-up interviews with participants who had put their family member into a nursing home since the original focus groups. Our goal was to hear their detailed accounts about how this change had taken place. A different use for follow-up individual interviews is to learn more about any perspectives that may have been underrepresented in the groups. Logistically, it may be more practical to track down several individual informants who fit the key characteristics rather than to put together an entire focus group of such people.

As these suggestions show, focus groups and individual interviews can be complementary techniques across a variety of different research designs. In particular, either of them can be used in either a preliminary or a follow-up capacity with the other. This illustrates the larger point that the goal of combining research methods is to strengthen the total research project, regardless of which method is the primary means of data collection.

Linking Focus Groups and Participant Observation

The principal benefit that focus groups have to offer to a project based on participant observation is a concentrated insight into participants' thinking on a topic. This can be especially useful when the research is entering a field site that differs sharply from his or her prior experience. In this case, the focus groups provide an initial exposure to the typical experiences and perspectives of those the researcher is about to observe. Given the well-known problems of gaining access to and establishing rapport in a new field site, preliminary focus groups with participants drawn from similar locations, other than the research setting itself, can often be quite useful.

Focus groups can also help in the selection of a site for participant observation. As with individual interviews, focus groups can be conducted with participants from each of several possible field settings to provide a basis for deciding among them. Comparing potential field settings to each other is especially useful in projects that utilize multiple field sites. Theoretical sampling is often an important element in selecting the comparisons that are built into a multisite case study (Yin, 1994), and preliminary focus groups at a variety of candidate sites can help determine which have the most potential for meaningful comparisons.

Focus groups can also contribute to theoretical sampling in observational studies that use Grounded Theory (Glaser & Strauss, 1967; Strauss & Corbin, 1990). In this approach, the researcher first completes a set of analyses at one site or with one population group and then searches for a theoretically motivated second sample that will provide the most informative comparison to what is already known. Focus groups would be a convenient source of insights into which kind of second sample would provide the most useful comparison. Alternatively, once the base set of observations was complete, the comparisons could be made via a set of follow-up focus groups with participants from theoretically selected subgroups. Using focus groups to make comparisons based on theoretical sampling lacks the richness of direct observation in natural settings, but this deficiency may be more than balanced by its practicality.

So far, the suggested uses of focus groups in combination with participant observation have concentrated on groups that are conducted outside the field site itself. One circumstance in which it would be desirable to draw the participants from the study site is at the end of the study as a way to test the researcher's understandings. This kind of "member checking" (Marshall & Rossman, 1995) can be accomplished by presenting the researcher's tentative conclusions to the participants as topics in a focus group discussion. Of course, these discussions provide only self-report data. In some cases, the participants may not have accurately analyzed the patterns in their own behavior, and in other cases they may have good reasons for refraining from public statements about every aspect of this behavior. In other words, discrepancies between the data from focus groups and participant observation do not inherently favor the participants' own statements in the focus groups. When such discrepancies do occur, however, they themselves may be an important form of data.

Linking Focus Groups and Surveys

Although focus groups have been recommended as a means to construct questionnaires for more than decade (e.g., Converse & Presser, 1986; Rossi, Wright, & Anderson, 1983), published accounts of how to put this advice into practice have begun to appear only recently (Fuller, Edwards, Vorakitphokatorn, & Sermsri, 1993; Hughes & DuMont, 1993; Laurie & Sullivan, 1991; O'Brien, 1993; Zeller, 1993). The present treatment cannot offer the depth that would be necessary for complete coverage of this subject. What I offer instead is an extended description of how focus groups can contribute to survey research projects, with the hope that their expanded use by social science survey practitioners will promote further growth in this area.

In their early history, survey researchers made more use of their potential respondents during the initial development of the questionnaire—for example, Thurstone's informants acted not only as judges of the proposed questions but also as the sources of the original item pool (Thurstone & Chave, 1929). As the number of available survey items has increased dramatically, so has the tendency to replicate existing items from other surveys. Aside from saving the work involved in developing new items, preexisting items typically carry some evidence of reliability and validity with them. Unfortunately, the evidence for validity may be quite weak, often consisting of nothing more than a nonzero correlation with a criterion measure that is itself of unknown validity. To the extent that the borrowed items were generated in "armchair" fashion, rather than through contact with the potential survey participants, they may yield a thoroughly reliable replication of an essentially invalid measure. Unfortunately, we have little basis for judging the magnitude of this problem, and we are rapidly reaching a point where most general population surveys consist entirely of items whose content has never been validated outside the confines of other surveys. Using focus groups to develop new survey items provides a way out of this circular situation.

There are three basic ways that focus groups can contribute to the creation of survey items: (a) by capturing all the domains that need to be measured in the survey, (b) by determining the dimensions that make up each of these domains, and (c) by providing item wordings that effectively convey the researcher's intent to the survey respondent. First, with regard to locating domains, focus groups can ensure that the researcher has as complete a picture of participants' thinking as possible rather than simply relying on the researcher's assumptions about what is relevant. Of course, other qualitative methods besides focus groups can provide this kind of insight about which domains need to be covered. For example, Bauman and Adair (1992) recount how ethnographic interviews helped them recognize role strain as an important factor that needed to be added to their study of social support among mothers who were caring for a chronically ill child. The general advantage of focus groups for this task undoubtedly stems from their ability to provide access to a wide range of perspectives in a rather short time. Because the development of the survey depends on this preliminary work, the ability to do focus groups relatively quickly can be a major asset.

Once the domains are recognized, either through the researcher's prior knowledge or qualitative contact with potential respondents, the second task is to determine a set of dimensions that will "cover" each domain. Focus groups are once again an efficient tool for this task because a relatively small number of groups can generate a large number of ideas about the categories of items that are needed to cover each questioning area. A similar advantage applies to the third way that focus groups can aid survey development—through insights into question wording. Although this is often cited as the primary use of focus groups for generating survey questions, I have placed it last to demonstrate the wider range of inputs that focus groups can generate. It is certainly the case, however, that group discussions can produce ways of expressing an idea that simultaneously resonate with the potential respondents while minimizing questions and confusions.

The three ways that focus groups can contribute to generating survey questions correspond to a potential for reducing three different kinds of errors. First, locating the necessary domains reduces specification error, which is a very serious problem in multivariate analyses, because omitting relevant variables can bias the estimates for the parameters that do get included in the model (Berry & Feldman, 1985). Second, generating items that appropriately cover a domain can reduce invalidity both by ensuring that the content of the questions fully covers the content of the domain and by making sure that the questions mean the same thing to the respondents as they do to the researcher. Finally, finding item wordings that are appropriate for the widest possible range of respondents not only improves validity but also reduces unreliability by minimizing differences in how the respondents interpret the questions.

Focus groups can also augment the pretesting that is necessary to evaluate a survey instrument. When the researchers are relatively unfamiliar with a given topic or when issues of language are a particular problem, it would be useful to hold a group discussion of the proposed items in crucial sections of the questionnaire prior to pretesting in the field. Knodel et al. (1984) have suggested that such groups make it much easier to detect when participants fail to understand a question as the researcher intended it. Pretesting with focus groups would not only locate such problems but also allow an immediate exploration of how to correct them.

A final way that focus groups can be of value in the preliminary work on a survey is by generating hypotheses. More times than I can count, survey researchers have told me that they used focus groups for the explicit purpose of generating survey items but then became excited to discover that the groups also gave them new ideas about how to analyze their data. Thus, inductive contacts with respondents can supplement deductive contacts with theory as a source of hypotheses.

Using focus groups to develop surveys is not without its dangers, however. In particular, for both the pretesting and the development of instruments it is important not to let a chance remark from one respondent either kill a good idea or push the researcher into a decision that is not supported by broader data. Given the vividness of the direct contact with the research participants (Axelrod, 1975), isolated incidents in focus groups can have disproportionate effects, even among researchers who earn their living through the power of generalizable samples. The goal in using preliminary focus groups or other qualitative data to supplement survey work should be to learn things that can guide one's work, not determine it.

At the later stages of a survey, when the data are in and the analysis begins, focus groups can again be of value through a follow-up data collection that pursues "exploratory" aspects of the analysis. This is especially important when the results are puzzling to the researchers. Too often, the tendency is to throw every possible variable into the analysis and then retreat to armchair speculation about what might have created the results. Asking the participants themselves is a better strategy. Did they understand and respond to the questions in the way the researchers intended? Did they consider factors that the researchers failed to question them about? Can they give a straightforward basis for their responses that can be tested as a hypothesis? The earlier examples of Knodel et al.'s (1987) research on changes in Thai fertility and my own research on social support among recent widows (Morgan, 1989) are both illustrations of this use of focus groups. Consequently, I have a simple answer for survey researchers who wonder why their respondents said what they did: "Why don't you ask them?"

These various suggestions show that focus groups have a considerable potential for contributing to survey research. If some of these suggestions have taken a more critical tone than those for other methods, it is largely because survey research has been so successful at establishing itself as a self-sufficient source of social science data. Such self-sufficiency, however, can become inbreeding. Given the importance of surveys to social science research, it makes sense not only to make use of every strength that they offer but also to take advantage of the strengths that other methods have to offer. Fortunately, survey researchers already have noted the value of combining their work with focus groups, and even the relatively small body of literature that exists in this area makes it one of the most thoroughly studied combinations of qualitative and quantitative methods.

Linking Focus Groups and Experiments

Although the application of focus groups to experiments was central to the original research program of Merton et al. (1990), this combination is almost totally absent from current experimental work in social psychology. If laboratory-based experiments have ignored the potential contributions of focus groups, however, applied experimental work, in the form of community-based intervention programs, has embraced focus groups wholeheartedly.

One of the chief applications of focus groups in community-based interventions was also one of the major uses that Merton et al. (1990) noted: specifying an effective stimulus. In an experimental context, this would mean using preliminary focus groups to define "manipulations" of independent variables. Because the success of community-based interventions depends on the effectiveness of their programs, the use of focus groups and other qualitative methods in the design of these programs makes eminently good sense. This is, of course, analogous to the use of focus groups in developing questions for survey interviews. In this case, however, the specific goals are to hear how the program's potential clients experience the issues in question and how they respond to potential interventions for addressing these issues. The larger goal is to increase the chance of designing a successful intervention. Such efforts have been especially prominent in various aspects of public health education under the heading of "social marketing" (Andreason, 1995). Indeed, social marketing often uses focus groups to design media campaigns (e.g., Bryant, 1990) in ways that are the direct descendants of Merton and Lazarsfeld's work to generate training manuals and propaganda films during World War II.

Another preliminary use for focus groups in applied experimentation is the selection of appropriate outcome measures. In particular, any attempt to assess the effectiveness of an intervention depends on selecting outcome measures that are likely to be sensitive to the treatment as delivered. Focus groups that give indications about the aspects of clients' behavior that are most likely to be modified will help in selecting outcome measures that can capture a program's real-world impacts.

If the attractiveness of focus groups as a tool in the design of community-based interventions is obvious, their advantages in the evaluation of such projects are even more self-evident. As a form of qualitative evaluation (Patton, 1990), focus groups help to understand experiences and responses of program participants. Krueger (1994) provides a thorough discussion of the uses of focus groups in relation to applied research in general and program evaluation in particular.

The use of focus groups within a program assessment framework once again features many of the benefits that Merton et al. (1990) described in their original description of group interviewing, including interpreting discrepancies between anticipated and actual effects, interpreting the ways that effects on subgroups may differ from the effects in the larger population, and interpreting the process involved in the actual production of intervention's effects. In the first case, if the intervention does not work as planned, then follow-up focus groups with the program participants can help to locate the reasons behind these problems. Regarding the second case, it is often the case that a program does not work equally well for all the clients it is supposed to serve, and focus groups with different categories of clients can help to locate why it works better for some types of clients than for others. Finally, focus groups have evaluation applications even when a program was a clear success. In particular, an explicit investigation of the sources of a program's success, by hearing the perspective of the program participants themselves, is wiser than simply assuming that the program worked for the reasons that its designers intended. In general, these applications all illustrate the strengths that focus groups as a qualitative method have for investigating the "how and why" of program success and failure (Yin, 1994).

Research involving the assessment of community-based interventions also points to one further way that focus groups can be joined with experimental research methods. In many cases, focus groups can be used with traditional quantitative evaluation tools to produce an especially effective combination of results. In particular, an effective way to communicate with policymakers about the results of complex statistical models is to combine statistical evidence with focus group accounts that provide a more accessible understanding of the ways that a particular program made a difference. The focus groups can thus help "put a human face" on the results from the quantitative analyses.

Summing Up

As noted at the outset of this chapter, there are a great many uses for focus groups, both in combination with other methods and as a self-contained source of qualitative data. We have come a long way from the days when focus groups were restricted to the role of preliminary, exploratory research. I do not, however, want to denigrate the value of focus groups for exploratory research. Exploration is a great strength of qualitative methods in general and focus groups in particular, so we should neither downplay this key contribution nor allow ourselves to be limited by it.

One way to make the case for moving beyond the use of focus groups as an exploratory technique is to draw attention to a whole series of possible research designs that are largely missing from this chapter: those in which focus groups serve as the primary means of data collection while other methods play a supplementary role. Given the relative newness of focus groups in the social sciences, it is hardly surprising that most of their existing combinations with other methods rely more heavily on the better known methods. Now that research using self-contained focus groups is becoming more common, however, we should be able to look forward to a whole new set of research designs that explore the ways that surveys, experiments, participant observation, and individual interviews can contribute to research that relies primarily on focus groups.

A final point should be made to connect this material to the comparison between focus groups and other qualitative methods in the previous chapter. Participant observation and individual interviewing could easily be used instead of focus groups in many of the multimethod combinations I have discussed, and there are undoubtedly circumstances in which these other qualitative methods would be superior to focus groups for this purpose. Although focus groups may have some advantages in combining with other methods, it is best not to overstate them. The argument for combining methods is fundamentally a plea for the mutual relevancy of all research methods rather than an assertion of the superiority of any one technique.

4. PLANNING AND RESEARCH
DESIGN FOR FOCUS GROUPS

This chapter addresses the planning that must be done prior to doing focus groups. Both it and the next chapter on how to conduct and analyze focus groups will have more emphasis on technical procedures. Such practicalities are an important aspect of any research technique, and focus groups do not differ greatly from other qualitative methods of data collection in this regard. In particular, the framework for the next two chapters is based on Kirk and Miller's (1986) general description of the four phases of qualitative research: planning, observation, analysis, and reporting.

Of these four phases in the life of a research project, this presentation will devote one entire chapter to the planning phase. I emphasize planning because this is the area where focus groups depart most from standard practices in other qualitative methods. The fact that they are group interviews is the source of most of these planning needs. In particular, the need to bring together several participants requires attention to who the participants are and how the researcher will interact with them as a group. Once the choices surrounding the format of the group interview are made, the subsequent observation, analysis, and reporting phases mostly pose issues that are already familiar to experienced qualitative researchers.

Before Starting

Three obvious factors that affect the ability to plan are ethical concerns, budget issues, and time constraints. In many respects, the ethical concerns in focus groups are similar to those raised in all qualitative research (Punch, 1986), but the specific concerns generated by focus groups also require attention (Smith, 1995). Issues concerning invasion of privacy are especially important whenever taping is the primary means of data collection. Actual audio and visual presentations of tapes are relatively rare in the social sciences, but they can be very tempting in the case of focus groups. No amount of accuracy in transcription will ever substitute for the excitement of actually listening to an emotional exchange among participants, and videotapes can be even more seductive. It is thus wise to decide up front who will hear or see the tapes. My advice would be to limit this access to the research staff; unless you know from the beginning that public presentation of the tapes will be an integral part of the research, it is best to rule out this option altogether.

One unique ethical issue in focus groups is the fact that what participants tell the researcher is inherently shared with other group participants as well. This raises serious invasion of privacy concerns and effectively limits the kinds of topics that the researcher can pursue. Such limitations are actually practical as well as ethical: It is not a productive use of focus groups to ask people to talk with discussion partners with whom they are not comfortable. In other words, most focus groups that involve an invasion of privacy are also a waste of the researcher's time. Note, however, that this argument does not necessarily apply to groups of self-acknowledged deviants, especially if they are members of deviant subcultures in which the informal equivalent of focus group discussions occur. That case requires the usual protection of participants, with the added assurance that all the participants in each discussion truly belong to the shared milieu.

Turning to budget issues as a factor in planning focus groups, one guideline is that marketing researchers often charge clients over $2,000 per group when participants come from the general population, and this figure may double when working with specialized groups of participants who are more difficult to recruit. If the research is being subcontracted to a marketing firm, this is what it will cost. If you are doing some of the work yourself, it will probably cost substantially less.

Major cost factors include salaries to moderators, travel to research sites, rental of research sites, payments to participants, and producing and transcribing tapes. Many of these costs are essentially fixed by the circumstances of the specific research project, but substantial savings are possible if the researcher has the time and skills necessary to perform the moderator function. This is especially true if the only alternative is hiring an outside moderator because these skills often have a price tag that is more in line with the resources of corporate clients rather than academics. One cost-saving compromise is to hire a moderator whose sole role is to conduct the groups and not to analyze the data. This not only takes advantage of the professional moderator's specific skills but also recognizes that the task of making sense of the data is best handled by those who will ultimately be responsible for its use. Even this compromise, however, requires that the research team allocate both time and money for working with the outside moderator to plan the project because both parties must have a truly shared understanding of the research objectives and procedures.

Social science research projects vary considerably in the time constraints that they place on focus groups. When the focus groups serve a specific purpose within a larger project, such as producing questions for a survey instrument or guiding the design of an intervention program, then such groups may need to be done on tight timelines. Typically, the time savings for such work comes from less detailed analyses; because the uses for the groups are quite explicit, the summary of their content is more straightforward. In these limited cases, the entire focus group project may be completed in just a few weeks. The kind of qualitative research that would satisfy journal reviewers or a dissertation committee, however, may require time for not only more detailed analyses of transcripts but also the possibility of returning to the field for more data.

In the planning phase, the design decisions themselves typically require at least 2 weeks—more if the project is complex or if the research team is inexperienced with the method. Furthermore, the recruitment of participants may be quite time-consuming, especially when using specialized populations or comparing multiple categories of participants. In the observation phase, although each group takes only a few hours, conducting two a day, or even five a week, can be a killing pace without either a very large staff or considerable reliance on outside services. Finally, in terms of analysis and reporting, transcript typing is slow, and transcript analysis is very time-consuming. Depending on the number of groups, the availability of the participants, and the kind of analysis intended for the transcripts, count on a project taking between 3 and 6 months (longer if the staff divide their time between this project and other commitments).

From the beginning, it is important to have realistic expectations not just with regard to budget and time but also in terms of the total amount of investigator effort that is necessary to produce the desired data. This is hardly a new problem, but because of the relative novelty of focus groups in social science research it deserves attention. The reputation that focus groups have in some circles as a "quick and cheap" technique is due to the very limited function to which they have too often been relegated: preliminary explorations to set the stage for "real" research. Indeed, Morgan and Krueger's (1993) catalog of myths about focus groups includes the idea that they are either quick or cheap. When pursued as a self-contained research technique, focus groups demand the same attention to detail as any other means of data collection. As is always the case, the quality of the data depends on the quality of the preparation: Careful planning cannot guarantee insightful results, but a cavalier approach to the design and execution of the research is almost certain to produce poor results.

Overview of Focus
Group Research Design

The planning for a focus group project includes a number of decisions about how the data will be collected. Considered in order of their impact on the nature of the data, the first decision concerns who will participate in the groups. The next decision determines how structured the groups will be, including the level of moderator involvement. After that, there are further decisions about the size of each group and the number of groups in the total project.

Over the years, a number of "rules of thumb" have evolved to capture the most common choices that researchers have made with regard to each of these decisions (Morgan, 1992a). According to these rules of thumb, focus group projects most often (a) use homogeneous strangers as participants, (b) rely on a relatively structured interview with high moderator involvement, (c) have 6 to 10 participants per group, and (d) have a total of three to five groups per project. Unfortunately, some people act as if these rules of thumb constitute a standard about how focus groups should be done rather than a descriptive summary of how they often are done. In reality, most projects have some elements that require special attention, and it may be relatively rare for a project to match all four of these criteria.

These rules of thumb are most useful as a point of departure in the planning process. With regard to the choice of who the participants will be, it could be useful to ask whether homogeneous strangers would best serve the purposes of this particular project. This leads directly to questions about whether mixed groups would be more productive than homogeneous groups for this research topic or whether it is even realistic to try to recruit groups of strangers in this particular research setting. A similar self-questioning would apply to each of the other rules of thumb: Would a less structured interview or a lower level of moderator involvement produce more productive discussions on this topic among these participants? Would smaller groups produce more detailed data from each participant or would larger groups produce a wider range of ideas? Would it take a larger number groups to cover the participants' range of experiences and opinions on this topic or are there reasons to believe that a smaller number of groups will be sufficient? For any given decision, this self-questioning may result in staying with the original rule of thumb. If these rules of thumb do indeed represent the most frequent choices, then this is hardly surprising. Even so, a choice to go with a rule of thumb still needs to be a careful decision that is based on the needs of the specific project. The remaining sections of this chapter will provide guidance on making such decisions.

Determining the Types of Participants

SAMPLING CONCERNS

In selecting participants for a focus group project, it is often more useful to think in terms of minimizing sample bias rather than achieving generalizability. Focus groups are frequently conducted with purposively selected samples in which the participants are recruited from a limited number of sources (often only one). Such "bias" is a problem only if ignored—that is, interpreting data from a limited sample as representing a full spectrum of experiences and opinions. If a particular recruitment source does limit the nature of the data that are available, then this forces the choice between living with those limitations or finding other sources of participants that will reduce these biases.

The shift away from an emphasis on generalizability also means a shift from random sampling toward theoretically motivated sampling. Random sampling is seldom of use in selecting participants for focus groups for at least two reasons. First, the small number of participants involved in most focus group projects makes it extremely unlikely that a sample of size 40 or so will be adequate to represent a larger population, regardless of random selection. Second, a randomly sampled group is unlikely to hold a shared perspective on the research topic and may not even be able to generate meaningful discussions. In contrast, the following section presents several reasons for selecting focus group participants through purposive or "theoretical" sampling (Glaser & Strauss, 1967; Patton, 1990).

HOMOGENEITY AND SEGMENTATION

The decision to control the group composition to match carefully chosen categories of participants is known as *segmentation*. Segmented samples are closely tied to the emphasis on homogeneity in the composition of focus groups. It is this homogeneity that not only allows for more free-flowing conversations among participants within groups but also facilitates analyses that examine differences in perspective between groups. For example, if sex differences affected either the participants' comfort in the discussion or the analyst's ability to make useful comparisons, then there would be advantages to conducting separate groups of men and women—that is, segmenting by sex.

When are segmented samples and homogeneous groups the most appropriate choice? The group composition should ensure that the participants in each group both have something to say about the topic and feel comfortable saying it to each other. Try asking whether these participants could easily discuss this topic in normal, day-to-day interaction. Participants must feel able to talk to each other, and wide gaps in social background or lifestyle can defeat this requirement. Note, however, that the goal is homogeneity in background and not homogeneity in attitudes. If all the participants share virtually identical perspectives on a topic, this can lead to a flat, unproductive discussion.

The most common background variables that are considered in running mixed versus segmented groups are sex, race, age, and social class. Whether the sexes interact differently in mixed groups is a longstanding research question (Thorne & Henley, 1975); therefore, that alone may convince some researchers to segment by sex. This concern is most acute, however, when the issues raised by a given topic correspond to differences in perspectives between men and women. Such differences in perspectives may either reduce the comfort level in the discussion or affect how clearly either perspective gets discussed. Similar remarks apply to race, although, given the rather selective integration of American society, there may be even more topics in which racial differences in perspective could become an issue during group discussions. Older and younger participants may also have difficulty communicating with each other either because they have different experiences with a topic or because similar experiences are filtered through different generational perspectives. Class differences reflect a general segregation of interaction in our society so that even when the participants have few overt class differences in their experiences they may still be uncomfortable discussing personal experiences in each other's presence. This last point illustrates a more general concern: It is not the actual differences among participants but whether they perceive each other to be different that determines their willingness to discuss a topic together.

I illustrate these points using my research on widowhood (Morgan, 1989), in which most of the participants were women in their sixties and seventies, but one group had two male participants and another group contained a very young widow. In both these cases, there was a moderate disruption in the flow of the discussion because the other participants went out of their way to be solicitous to the "outsiders" in their group. All the groups, however, were quite mixed with regard to social class and this had little noticeable impact because these widows explicitly maintained that their bereavement created a fundamental similarity that overshadowed the differences in their backgrounds. In other words, their shared beliefs determined what made another's experience similar or different.

The choice between mixing and separating categories of participants also occurs when the participants occupy different social roles with regard to a topic. For example, the difference between fathers and mothers in a discussion of child-rearing practices is not just a difference between men and women. This issue is particularly common in organizations, in which individuals in various positions have routine patterns of what they do and do not discuss together. Differences in authority or status are particularly likely to create this problem, and such differences may occur in the general community as well as in organizations. There are strong arguments (Morgan & Krueger, 1993) against mixing categories of participants across authority or status lines, either due to ethical issues or because of the high probability that the discussion will be uncomfortable at best and conflict-ridden at worst.

Using groups that are segmented by background or role-based differences has the cost of requiring more groups because it takes a certain minimum number of groups within each category to observe that category's range of responses to a topic. Using multiple segmentation criteria makes the decisions about group composition more like an experimental design. Knodel (1993) describes a useful example of such a study.

The general strategy in using complex, segmented designs is to create a variety of internally homogeneous groups that capture a wide range of potentially distinct perspectives (Kitzinger, 1994a). Unfortunately, this approach can also make the data collection quite expensive and the analysis quite complex. One way to address this issue during the planning phase of the research is to try one pretest group that is mixed and then compare it to other groups that separate the categories in question. Comparing these discussions should reveal the comfort level in mixed groups.

STRANGERS VERSUS ACQUAINTANCES

A final decision in determining the group composition involves seeking out strangers versus allowing acquaintances to participate together. The rule of thumb favors strangers because, although acquaintances can converse more readily, this is often due to their ability to rely on the kind of taken-for-granted assumptions that are exactly what the researcher is trying to investigate (Agar & MacDonald, 1995). This problem is even more severe when the assumptions among acquaintances include invisible boundaries around the subjects that they have tacitly agreed not to discuss.

The notion that focus groups must consist of strangers, however, is certainly a myth (Morgan & Krueger, 1993). In fact, social scientists routinely conduct focus groups in organizations and other naturally occurring groups in which acquaintanceship is unavoidable. Furthermore, working with prior acquaintances can help the researcher deal with issues of self-disclosure (Jarrett, 1993). The real issue is that strangers and acquaintances can generate different group dynamics, which may lead a researcher to different choices, depending on the nature of the research goals.

Where differences in group dynamics are not an issue, practical concerns may govern the choice between strangers and acquaintances. In some cases, it may be almost impossible to recruit a full group of acquaintances (e.g., among service recipients); in other cases, it may be almost impossible to avoid it (e.g., in organizational settings). For these circumstances, decisions should rely on the basic criterion of whether a particular group of participants can comfortably discuss the topic in ways that are useful to the researcher.

RECRUITMENT ISSUES

To this point, this discussion has concentrated on determining the content of the sample, but an equally important set of issues concerns the recruitment of that sample. I have even argued that inadequate recruitment efforts are the single most common source of problems in focus group research projects (Morgan, 1995). Simply locating participants and getting them to agree to show up is often not enough; instead, it is essential to develop careful procedures that ensure that enough participants actually do show up for each group.

Projects that call for specific categories of participants require special recruitment efforts. Telephone screening interviews are one useful approach. This involves making phone calls, through either "random-digit dialing" or a predetermined list, and then asking a very short questionnaire to see if there is anyone in the household who both fits the recruitment category and is interested in participating. Such screening is more than just a mechanism for locating participants because homogeneity may be vital for the group's ability to share a discussion of the research topic. Even if only one of the participants fails to share some crucial characteristic, the discussion can get totally off track. If homogeneity is a major concern, then a further screening questionnaire can be administered to potential participants as they arrive for the discussion. Be warned, however, that screening questionnaires do run the risk of alerting participants to the topic of the research—or at least creating such expectations, whether they are accurate or not. When working with highly specialized categories of participants, recruitment procedures have to be equally specialized. In particular, it may be necessary to use substantial cash incentives to recruit top-level executives or others with unusual expertise; payments of $100 per person in such sessions are not uncommon. In community samples, marketers typically pay participants $25 to $50. Fortunately, there are many nonmonetary incentives for participating in focus groups (Krueger, 1994). In particular, if the research has an external sponsor that is meaningful to the participants (such as a popular community organization), involvement with this sponsor may substitute for a cash incentive. In dealing with uncertainty about incentives or other difficulties in the recruitment process, one general strategy is to conduct a few key informant interviews on the subject of recruitment—even qualitative researchers occasionally need to be reminded of the value of getting their participants' perspectives on a problem.

Determining the Level of Group Structure

Choices about interview standardization and moderator involvement go together to determine how structured the group discussion will be. Interview standardization refers to whether the same questions are asked of every group—that is, the extent to which the content of the interview is either predetermined or flexible. Moderator involvement refers to the management of the group dynamics—that is, the extent to which the moderator either controls the discussion or allows relatively free participation. Although there are various strategies for combining different degrees of interview standardization and moderator involvement (Morgan, 1992a), most projects tend to set both of them at comparable levels, which can be referred to as more structured or less structured approaches.

MORE STRUCTURED GROUPS

More structured approaches to focus groups are especially useful when there is a strong, preexisting agenda for the research. Both a standardized interview and a higher level of moderator involvement contribute to meeting this set agenda. When the project begins with a strong sense of what the research questions are, then a standardized interview will make sure that all the groups discuss these issues in a relatively comparable fashion. In addition, a higher level of moderator involvement will keep the discussion concentrated on the topics that interest the researchers rather than extraneous issues. Examples of goals that often rely on more structured approaches include providing inputs to other research efforts, such as program designs or survey content; making consistent comparisons across all the groups in a set; or comparing the thinking of a new set of participants with a previous set of groups.

The most obvious problem with more structured approaches is that a narrow set of questions or a motivated moderator may well produce equivalently limited data. Worse, it may be difficult to know that this is the case. Once participants sense that there is a distinct agenda for the discussion and that the moderator is there to enforce that agenda, then they are likely to acquiesce in all but the most extreme circumstances. More structured approaches thus pose a trade-off between more ability to hear about what interests the researchers and less ability to be sure that this is what actually matters to the participants themselves.

LESS STRUCTURED GROUPS

Less structured approaches to focus groups are especially useful for exploratory research. When the basic issues are poorly understood or existing knowledge is based on researcher-imposed agendas, then an unstandardized interview guide will provide the opportunity to hear the interests of the participants themselves in each group. In addition, minimizing the moderator's involvement in the discussion will give the participants more opportunity to pursue what interests them. What makes less structured focus groups such a strong tool for exploratory research is the fact that a group of interested participants can spark a lively discussion among themselves without much guidance from either the researcher's questions or the moderator's direction. In other words, if the goal is to learn something new from the participants, then it is best to let them speak for themselves.

A major disadvantage of less structured groups is that they are more difficult to compare from group to group. In particular, topics will come up in some groups and not in others. This difference in the topics that are raised from group to group makes the data more difficult to analyze than the well-ordered discussions that more structured approaches produce. The trade-off with less structured approaches is thus between a greater ability to learn about the participants' perspectives in their own words and less ability to pursue any aspect of these perspectives in a consistent fashion.

I illustrate the different uses for more structured and less structured approaches through a comparison of two studies I did with people who were caring for a family member with Alzheimer's disease (Morgan, 1992b). In one study, I used a more structured approach to compare the decision-making processes of caregivers who had brought their family members in for a diagnosis when the symptoms were either relatively mild or more severe. The goal in that study was to pinpoint the influence of several well-known factors in the caregivers' decision-making processes. To accomplish this, a structured interview guide walked the caregivers through the history of their decision making, and the moderator controlled the discussion to be sure that every caregiver had a roughly equal chance to tell his or her story.

In the other study, I used a less structured approach to compare caregivers who had placed their family member in an institution, such as a nursing home, with those who were still providing care in the community. The goals in that study were exploratory because relatively little was known about family caregiving in nursing homes; therefore, we wanted to compare the perspectives of community-based and nursing home-based caregivers. The interview guide in that study simply asked to hear as much as possible about what made caregiving either easier or harder, and the moderators minimized their direct involvement in the groups.

THE "FUNNEL" AS A COMPROMISE APPROACH

To this point, I have contrasted more structured and less structured approaches to focus groups as a way to emphasize the need to make research design choices about standardized versus unstandardized interview guides and high versus low levels of moderator involvement. It is also possible, however, to design a compromise between the two by using what is known as a funnel strategy. In a funnel-based interview, each group begins with a less structured approach that emphasizes free discussion and then moves toward a more structured discussion of specific questions. The funnel analogy matches an interview with a broad, open beginning and a narrower, more tightly controlled ending. This compromise makes it possible to hear the participants' own perspectives in the early part of each discussion as well as their responses to the researcher's specific interests in the later part of the discussion.

Although a funnel seems to offer the best of both worlds, it can be harder to achieve than either a more structured or a less structured approach. Blending the unstandardized opening with later, fixed questions requires care to find both a good starting point and a successful transition to the more controlled set of topics. Furthermore, shifting from a less involved to a more involved moderator style requires avoiding either an overly directive moderator style in the beginning or a nondirective style later on. Funnel designs thus work best in projects that truly need a combination of more structured and less structured data, and they are unlikely to "save" a project in which the researchers are simply uncertain about what kind of data they need.

Determining the Size of Groups

The amount that each participant has to contribute to the group is a major factor in decisions about group size. If the participants have a low level of involvement with the topic, it may be difficult to maintain an active discussion in a smaller group. Another key factor is how much detail the researchers need to hear from each participant. Small groups also run the risk of being less productive because they are so sensitive to the dynamics among the individual participants. In particular, the functioning of the group as a whole can easily be disrupted by friendship pairs, "experts," or uncooperative participants. Small groups thus work best when the participants are likely to be both interested in the topic and respectful of each other. In addition, small groups are more useful when the researcher desires a clear sense of each participant's reaction to a topic simply because they give each participant more time to talk.

Larger groups have a different set of problems that may limit their productivity. In particular, it is typically more difficult to manage their discussions, and this is especially true when the participants are highly involved in the topic. In practice, large groups can easily break up into small conversations among neighbors around the table, or people may start talking at once; either of these problems implies a loss of data because such conversations are very difficult to tape. Consequently, large groups typically require a higher level of moderator involvement, and it takes an experienced moderator to control them without engaging in continual efforts at discipline. As previously noted, however, such high levels of moderator involvement are not desirable for some research purposes.

One practical consideration is that, whatever size is selected, it is important to over-recruit to cover for no-shows. The common rule of thumb is to over-recruit by 20%, although the actual extent of over-recruitment depends on who the participants are, whether they are being paid for their participation, where the groups are conducted, and how vital the desired group size is for the overall design of the research.

Combining both practical and substantive considerations helps to clarify the basis for the rule of thumb size that specifies a range of 6 to 10. Below 6, it may be difficult to sustain a discussion; above 10, it may be difficult to control one. Even within this range, choices may still be necessary. For some topics, such as those in which participants have either relatively high or relatively low levels of involvement, there could be a world of difference in the dynamics for a group of 6 versus a group of 10. Also, one should not feel imprisoned by either this lower or upper boundary. I have conducted groups of 3 highly involved participants that would have been unmanageable at size 6, and I have led discussions in naturally occurring groups of 15 to 20 in which the process was quite orderly. Ultimately, both the purposes of the research and the constraints of the field situation must be taken into account.

Determining the Number of Groups

Although I have held off discussing the number of groups until last, this is not because this topic is less important than the others. In particular, the number of groups in the project will be the primary determinant of how much data the research produces. The number of groups also has a direct impact on the size and structure of the research team. Conducting many groups almost ensures the need for a larger research staff, the only other alternative being to extend the data collection and analysis over a longer period of time.

The basis for the rule of thumb that projects should consist of three to five groups comes from a claim that more groups seldom provide meaningful new insights. In both the social sciences (e.g., Zeller, 1993) and marketing (e.g., Calder, 1977), this is frequently summarized as the ability to stop collecting data when the moderator can accurately anticipate what will be said next in a group. Seasoned qualitative researchers will recognize this as another way of expressing the goal of "saturation" (Glaser & Strauss, 1967)—that is, the point at which additional data collection no longer generates new understanding.

Whether three to five groups will be adequate for saturation, however, is an issue that depends on many factors. Probably the most important determinant of the number of groups is the variability of the participants both within and across groups. Within groups, projects that bring together more heterogeneous participants will typically need more total groups because the diversity in the group often makes it more difficult to sort out coherent sets of opinions and experiences. Across groups, projects that compare several distinct population segments will typically require more total groups to achieve saturation within each segment.

Another factor that affects the number of groups is the degree of structure in the interviews. In general, projects that use less standardized interviews and lower levels of moderator involvement require more groups. The reason is that both of these factors increase the variability from group to group.

A different set of issues concerns the sheer availability of participants. If there are few potential participants available or if they are highly dispersed, then it is wisest to run several groups of smaller size. This is implicit in the criterion of saturation because it is necessary to compare the discussions from several groups to determine whether the participants are repeating what was said in earlier groups.

Regardless of the circumstances, collecting only one group creates severe problems. The problem with having only one group is that it is impossible to tell when the discussion reflects either the unusual composition of that group or the dynamics of that unique set of participants. Even when there are data from just two groups, if what they say is highly similar then this provides much safer ground in concluding that group dynamics were not responsible for this content. Also, if the discussions in the two groups differ, then this is a fair warning that saturation has not been achieved. A different version of the same problem occurs in projects that use multiple segments because the substantive content of the group's discussion is confounded with its unique composition and dynamics. There should thus be more than one group in each segment, which will obviously increase the total number of groups in groups that use multiple segments.

In general, the goal is to do only as many groups as are required to provide a trustworthy answer to the research question due to the costs involved in conducting more groups. These costs involve not only additional efforts in recruitment and data collection but also additional coding and analysis efforts with a larger number of transcripts. There are dangers in plans that call for using a bare minimum number of groups, however, because this can make the project as a whole vulnerable when a single group fails (e.g., because not enough participants show up or because a group is so unusual as to be of dubious utility). The safest advice is to determine a target number of groups in the planning stage but to have a flexible alternative available if more groups are needed.

Summing Up

Clearly, there are a great many issues to be considered in planning for focus groups. This chapter has only touched on a set of general issues that are likely to affect nearly all focus groups; any specific research project will confront many more issues than these. In particular, several of the issues covered in the following chapter have additional planning implications. Just as important, it would be unfortunate to give the impression that planning is a discrete stage in the research project. Planning is not something that is over and done by a given point, with a totally new set of concerns waiting to replace it. Even when the goal is to do a quick and inexpensive set of focus groups, this does not eliminate the need for planning. Indeed, this chapter should have made it painfully obvious that the only way to take advantage of the flexibility of focus groups is through a diligent effort at prior planning!

5. CONDUCTING AND ANALYZING FOCUS GROUPS

This chapter takes up the questions of how to do focus groups and what to do with the data they produce. Like the previous chapter, this chapter has a practical orientation to the technical aspects of focus groups. Continuing Kirk and Miller's (1986) general description of the four phases of qualitative research, this chapter turns from planning to observation, analysis, and reporting. The chapter begins with a broad overview from Merton et al. (1990) of the researcher's goals throughout the entire interview process. Their summary is particularly useful at this point because it emphasizes issues that bridge the gap between planning and conducting the research.

Merton et al. (1990) present four broad criteria for the effective focus group interview: It should cover a maximum range of relevant topics; provide data that are as specific as possible, foster interaction that explores the participants' feelings in some depth, and take into account the personal context that participants use in generating their responses to the topic. They summarize these criteria as range, specificity, depth, and personal context.

Under the heading of range, Merton et al. (1990) note that successful groups discuss a range of topics that not only covers the issues that researchers already know to be important but also may bring up issues that the researchers had not anticipated. Too often, researchers inadvertently narrow the discussion by implicitly assuming which issues are important. For example, in our research on heart attacks (Morgan & Spanish, 1985), we carefully avoided all mention of the term "risk factor." By not cuing the participants on this concept, we were able to use it to check the range of issues that they discussed and to observe the extent to which their own conceptions of what caused and prevented heart attacks introduced issues that went beyond standard medical lists of risk factors.

Merton et al. (1990) emphasize specificity to direct the focus group discussions toward concrete and detailed accounts of the participants' experiences. I presented a similar argument in Chapter 3, advocating questions about participants' experiences with a topic. It can be all too easy for participants to drift off into generalities, but an emphasis on hearing about the participants' experiences can help counteract this tendency.

Merton et al. (1990) stress depth to ensure the participants' involvement with the material they are discussing. As with specificity, the goal is to avoid a discussion of vague generalities. Techniques for guaranteeing depth are more necessary when the participants are not involved with a topic; this is less problematic with participants who are highly involved with a topic because they already have a motivation to share opinions and experiences. In either case, an emphasis on sharing personal experiences can generate a level of depth that draws the entire group into the discussion.

The final criterion for observations that Merton et al. (1990) offer is attention to the personal context from which individual remarks arise— what is it about a particular participant that leads him or her to express things in a particular way? Once again, Chapter 3 introduced a similar emphasis, under the heading of perspective. Perspectives and personal contexts may be based on the social roles and categories that the participants occupy; they may also be rooted in more individual experiences. Either way, the point of doing a group interview is to bring a number of different perspectives into contact. Until they interact with others on a topic, individuals are often simply unaware of their own implicit perspectives. Moreover, the interaction in the group may present the need to explain or defend one's perspective to someone who thinks about the world differently. Using focus groups to create such interactions gives the researcher a set of observations that is difficult to obtain through other methods.

Determining the Interview Content

Any attempt to gather observations through interviewing requires attention to the concrete issues of interview content. The goal here is to construct an interview that covers the particular topic at hand while generating observations that satisfy Merton et al.'s (1990) four criteria for an effective focus group.

The most obvious constraint on interview content is the fact that a typical discussion lasts 1 or 2 hours. Safe advice would be to set the length at 90 minutes, but tell participants that the discussion will run 2 hours—this half-hour cushion avoids the disruption of the group dynamics from either "late arrivers" or "early leavers." Within this time span, it is important to maintain the focus and not explore too many topics. For an unstructured group, this might mean just two broadly stated topics or questions. In a more structured group, the limit should probably be four or five distinct topics or questions, with preplanned probes under each major topic.

For more structured groups, it is useful to organize the discussion topics into a guide that the moderator follows in more or less the same order from group to group. The structure that a guide imposes on discussions is valuable both in channeling the group interaction and in making comparisons across groups in the analysis phase of the research. A good guide creates a natural progression across topics with some overlap between the topics—an artificial compartmentalization of the discussion defeats the purpose of using group interaction. An additional value to creating a guide is to ensure consensus among the various members of the research team with regard to which topics are to be covered at what level of detail.

One common form of guide is based directly on questions. This format is most popular in more structured approaches to focus groups because the very act of asking questions signals the moderator's basic control over the content and direction of the group's discussion. A more flexible format is to organize the guide around a set of discussion topics that are only loosely phrased as questions—for example, "One of the things that we are especially interested in is _____. What can you tell us about that?" In reality, if the topics in the guide are on target, it often is unnecessary to ask an explicit question because the discussion can be turned toward an emerging topic with a cue such as "That's something we're definitely interested in hearing more about. What can any of you tell us about that?"

It is also important to take the concept of a guide quite literally, avoiding the tendency to follow a predetermined order of topics in a rigid fashion.

In particular, it is important to avoid what Merton et al. (1990) term the fallacy of adhering to fixed questions. Instead, the moderator needs to be free to probe more deeply where necessary, skip over areas that have already been covered, and follow completely new topics if they arise. It is perfectly acceptable for the guide to produce occasional moderator interventions such as "Let's hold off on that right now, since we'll be getting to it in a little while." If such remarks become a frequent feature of the discussions, however, it is necessary either to revise the guide or to apply it less rigidly. With a good guide and perhaps a little pretesting, the discussion should flow from topic to topic. If, instead, the moderator has to work hard to force attention to a topic or to keep attention from shifting to another topic, this should be a warning that there is something out of synch between the guide and the participants' perspectives on the topic.

The problems encountered in adhering too rigidly to a guide reinforce the point that even structured interviews should not be moderator-dominated discussions. The role of being a moderator should not be that of an interviewer. The title "moderator" highlights this role's orientation toward helping out someone else's discussion. Similarly, the concept of a "guide" emphasizes that the researcher's list of questions or topics should help channel the discussion without necessarily forcing the group into a predetermined mold. In essence, the moderator uses the guide as a resource to maintain the balance between the researcher's focus and the group's discussion.

Too often, researchers who are new to focus groups assume that it is the moderator who produces the data. In reality, the interview guide has at least as much influence on the content of the group discussion as does the moderator (Morgan, 1995). Hence, when I train novice moderators, I pay as much attention to constructing a good guide as to managing the actual group dynamics. The reason is that an effective guide can produce a discussion that manages itself, whereas an ineffective guide can produce problems that no amount of moderating skill can fix.

Moderating the Group

Both high- and low-moderator-involvement sessions often begin the same way. In either case, it is important to open the session by introducing the topic in an honest but fairly general fashion. There are two reasons for beginning at the level of generalities. First, participants may not be able to follow a researcher's detailed thinking on a topic. Second, they may be looking for some sense of purpose and direction, and a detailed introduction can lead them to restrict and channel their discussion. A combination of these two problems can be deadly.

The introduction of the topic is typically accompanied by a few ground rules: only one person speaking at a time, no side conversations among neighbors, everyone participating with no one dominating, and so on. It is wise to keep both the introduction and the instructions as brief as possible. A lengthy set of instructions can easily get the group off to a bad start because it creates an expectation that the moderator will be telling the group what to do. Instead, the goal should be to make the group members feel responsible for generating and sustaining their own discussion.

The best introduction is often the honest admission that the researcher is there to learn from them, but do not carry this attitude to the extreme of faking ignorance. Participants are unlikely to be fooled by this, and it runs the risk of producing a series of lectures from newly appointed experts rather than an open exchange of experiences and opinions. The point of interviewing the participants is to learn from them, so express the goals for the session in those terms. In low-moderator-involvement sessions, such an introduction provides a good justification for retiring from the discussion. In high-moderator-involvement sessions, it creates a good basis for probing even the most seemingly obvious of statements.

BEGINNING THE DISCUSSION

For the early part of the group discussion, it is helpful to think of the difference between an "ice-breaker" question and a true "discussion-starter" question. In the ice-breaker question, each person around the table gives a very brief self-introduction. This helps set the mood for the group as a whole. For example, if the researcher desires a lighter touch in the discussion, then the introduction can include a request to "tell us something about what you like to do for fun." In contrast, discussion-starter questions present the basic topic for the session and throw the discussion open to the group as a whole.

In starting the actual discussion, a central objective is to get each participant to give some meaningful response or opening statement. Hence, a key feature of the discussion-starter question is that one should easily be able to respond to it. More to the point, it should be something that all the participants will be interested in. If the discussion-starter question meets these criteria, then it will be simple for the moderator to track who has given an opening statement and to facilitate the discussion by reminding the group that the goal is to hear from everyone. This is a good example of how a proper set of interview questions can be as important as well-developed moderating skills. Discussion-starter questions also help in dealing with latecomers because an approachable question makes it easier to integrate them into this phase of the group. In addition, this stage provides an easy cutoff, allowing the moderator to exclude anyone who arrives after the opening statements have ended and the subsequent discussion has begun.

A more subtle advantage of getting each person to make an opening statement is that it helps to deter "groupthink" (Janis, 1982)—that is, the tendency for dissenters to suppress their disagreements in favor of maintaining consensus in the group. Discussion-starter questions that encourage opening statements are a way of getting everyone on record with their different experiences and opinions before a consensus emerges. One way to ensure this process is to ask each person to take a couple of minutes to make written notes prior to responding to the discussion starter question— essentially creating a "nominal group" (Stewart & Shamdasani, 1990). There is something about the process of writing things down that reinforces a person's commitment to contributing these thoughts to the group, even in the face of apparent disapproval. Having written statements available also gives the moderator a legitimate basis for asking for input from those who have not said anything yet.

Beginning with a general question that emphasizes the participants' interests lets the researcher hear the participants' perspectives. By tapping into the topic from the participants' point of view rather than starting with the researcher's manifest interests, there is an opportunity to discover new ways of thinking about the issues. This kind of opening also produces direct evidence about the amount of consensus and diversity in the group—information that is of value not only for the subsequent analysis but also for the immediate task of managing the upcoming discussion. Even when an apparent consensus does emerge in this early discussion, the material from the opening statements gives the other participants as well as the moderator a basis for probing the strength and the breadth of the consensus.

CONTINUING AND CONCLUDING THE DISCUSSION

How to move from the opening to the body of the discussion will depend, in large part, on the level of moderator involvement. When a general discussion-starter question serves as the top of the funnel in a more structured group, the goal is not so much to get a full answer to this question as to set up an agenda of topics to be covered within the limits of a flexible guide. Therefore, after perhaps 10 minutes of open discussion the moderator will create an opportunity to introduce the first substantive topic on the guide: "One thing I've heard several people mention is _____. I wonder what the rest of you have to say about that?" Alternately, if the first topic in the interview guide has not been raised yet: "One thing that I'm surprised no one has mentioned is _____. Does it matter or not?" This kind of tracking back and forth between what the group brings up and what the guide calls for is not limited to the early part of the discussion. Topics that are mentioned in the opening discussion need to be remembered and used to segue into later topics in the guide: "I recall that some of you mentioned something a little different earlier, and I wonder how things like _____ fit into the picture?"

Using material that participants have raised earlier as a basis for moving to another segment of the guide is especially useful when the discussion slows down. Not every group will be equally interested in every topic in a guide. When the discussion flags, a moderator who has tracked the connections between the participants' conversations and the guide can easily redirect the discussion toward material in which the group has already indicated its interest.

Just as the transition between individual opening statements and actual group discussion provides a clear beginning to the group, it is also a good idea to provide a clear indication of when the session is ending. In low-moderator-involvement groups, the simple return of the moderator to the table provides this cue. In high-moderator-involvement groups, asking each person to give a final summary statement is a useful technique. A sense that the final statement will not be interrupted or challenged may allow a participant to make a contribution that he or she has been holding back from the open discussion. Some moderators take advantage of this potential new material by letting the informal discussion continue after the formal group is over, with the tape continuing to roll during this more informal exchange. If there is good reason to believe that individuals have not expressed their full opinions, then an additional possibility is to call each participant a day or two after the session for a brief thank-you and the opportunity to express "any other thoughts that may have occurred to you."

CONDUCTING LOW-MODERATOR-INVOLVEMENT GROUPS

Specific techniques for moderating high-moderator-involvement focus groups are well described elsewhere (e.g., Goldman & McDonald, 1987; Greenbaum, 1993; Krueger, 1994). Advice on low-moderator focus groups is less common, however. Perhaps this is because such groups are primarily of interest to social science researchers. Be that as it may, I devote somewhat more space to concrete advice about how to moderate low-moderator-involvement groups.

With low levels of moderator involvement, the discussion of the broad discussion-starter question may be the basis for the entire interview! For example, my research on widowhood (Morgan, 1989) used focus groups that were relatively short (1 hour) and consisted of only a single topic: "What sorts of things have made it easier for you and what sorts of things have made it harder?" Even when a low-moderator-involvement group does use an interview guide that specifies two or three large topics or questions, these broad areas will typically overlap a great deal. Allowing for overlaps between topics is illustrated by the focus groups that Margaret Spanish and I (Morgan & Spanish, 1985) conducted on beliefs about heart attacks. These interviews lasted about 90 minutes and began with opening statements that had each participant tell a brief story about someone he or she knew who had had a heart attack. The rest of the discussion consisted of two topics: "Who has heart attacks and why?" and "What causes and what prevents heart attacks?" If the first half of the discussion ran down to a natural conclusion, then we simply introduced the second topic; if the first half ran overtime, the overlap with the second topic allowed us to break into the discussion and redirect it with a minimum of disruption.

In terms of managing the group discussion itself, many descriptions of what moderators do make it seem as if the discussion would collapse without the active presence of a moderator. The most frequently cited justifications for high involvement have to do with controlling the interaction in the group, including getting irrelevant discussions back on the track, restarting discussion when the group runs dry, ensuring that groupthink does not stifle opinions that differ from those of the majority, cutting off overly dominant participants, engaging overly reticent participants, and so on. Most of these problems, however, can be handled by the group itself with a minimal level of moderator involvement.

Over the years, I have developed several explicit techniques for getting groups to solve problems through self-management. Each of these themes would be introduced at the beginning of the session by the moderator, who would then retire to a separate table to take notes and manage the tape recorder. The following are sample techniques and instructions, but note that there is no need to drum them into the participants—if the group is larger than four or five, it is virtually assured that someone will remember and apply an instruction.

- Legitimate the members' responsibility to manage the discussion: "If you tend to get off the track, someone will usually pull the group back to [the topic]—we'll jump in if we have to, but usually one of you takes care of that for us." Note that here and throughout, the underlying strategy is to create a "self-fulfilling prophecy" (another of Merton's contributions). In other words, your instructions should model the behavior that you want the group to adopt.

- Cue them on how to handle common problems: "If the group runs out of things to say, just remember that what we're interested in is [research topic] and we want to hear as many different things about this as possible. So what usually happens is that someone will think of something that hasn't come up yet and then that will restart the discussion."

- Emphasize that you want as many different perspectives as possible: "If your experience is a little different from what others are saying, then that is exactly when we want to hear from you. Often someone says, 'I guess my experience is different from everyone else's . . .' and then they find out that the same things have happened to other people too, but no one else would have mentioned it if someone didn't start the ball rolling."

- Get them to use questions to direct the flow of interaction: "If someone hasn't really joined in, or you seem to be hearing from the same people all the time, try asking a question to someone who hasn't spoken as much. We have everyone say a little bit about themselves in the first part of the discussion, so listen to what the others say at the start. Then, later on, you can use this information to ask someone a question that will draw them back into the discussion."

- Emphasize hearing about their experiences. Not everyone is willing to state or defend an opinion, but most people are willing to tell their stories: "We want to hear as many stories as possible. Even if you think your experience is just like everyone else's, don't just say, 'I agree.' We want to hear your story, because there's always something unique in each person's own experiences."

- Stress that all experiences are equally important to you: "We need to hear as many different things from as many of you as time allows. There really aren't right or wrong answers in this area—if there were, we'd go to experts and they'd tell us the answers. Instead, we're here to learn from your experiences."

Conducting low-moderator-involvement groups does not mean that the research has no focus at all. As the previous example of questions from our research on heart attacks illustrated, there typically are a set of key topics, and the moderator can steer the group members toward those topics if they do not spontaneously cover them. Of course, the absence of spontaneous discussion also represents data. A lack of spontaneous discussion, however, should not be confused with a true lack of interest in a topic, and this is especially so when a low level of moderator involvement reduces the consistency in the topics that arise from group to group.

The fact that low-moderator-involvement discussions differ so much from group to group also gives the researcher an opportunity to modify the content of the questions as the research proceeds. In the most common case, material that has been well covered in earlier sessions will be given only limited attention in later groups (to assure their similarity with previous groups on these issues), whereas other topics will be pursued in greater detail. For example, a single question from the earlier discussion guide may expand to become the topic for an entire set of new discussions, with a new guide elevating the various points made in the earlier discussions to become separate discussion topics in the follow-up groups. In other cases, new topics may emerge during the original groups, leading to additional groups that address these further issues in more detail. This pattern of revising the direction of the research as the data gathering and analysis proceeds is in line with the general approach of grounded theory (Glaser & Strauss, 1967; Strauss & Corbin, 1990).

It is certainly true that higher levels of moderator involvement produce greater consistency across groups, but such consistency is not a goal in its own right. Instead, it is one potential means of meeting the goals of the larger research design. In particular, when the purpose of the research is frankly exploratory, then a design that relies on low moderator involvement and an evolving set of research topics is likely to be a good match. In contrast, when the purpose of the research is either to answer predetermined research questions or to make comparisons across groups from different segments, this is likely to call for the greater degree of consistency that goes with higher levels of moderator involvement.

Site Selection and Data Collection

The first consideration in setting up the actual observation is the selection of a site to conduct the focus groups. The site must balance the needs of participants and the needs of the researcher; there is little use for sites where participants will not be comfortable or where it is not possible to record the session. The most likely alternatives are conference rooms in a public facility such as a community center, library, or school. Other alternatives are at the researcher's office or in the participants' homes. In larger cities, it is often possible to rent specialized focus group facilities at a cost of approximately $200 to $300 per session. These facilities resemble a comfortably furnished group dynamics laboratory, with built-in microphones, video cameras, and a "viewing room" behind a one-way mirror. In addition, such facilities typically offer other related services such as recruitment of the participants. Because this is where a majority of marketing focus groups are conducted, these facilities usually list themselves as marketing services in telephone directories.

The most basic element of the site is a table for the participants, with circular or rectangular conference tables being the most common options. If the moderator is placed at one end of a rectangular table, this will produce a U-shaped arrangement of the participants. This arrangement is useful for videotaping because the camera can be placed behind the moderator to yield a facial view of the participants. In addition, having the moderator at the head of the table gives some control over individuals' level of participation. This involves placing those who are likely to be less talkative directly across from the moderator, making it easier for the moderator to send nonverbal encouragement to them. Similarly, placing those who might dominate the discussion on either side of the moderator makes it easier to lean past them to encourage the participation of the rest of the group.

The principal means of capturing observations in a focus group is through audio taping, and any choices about physical facilities must be made with tape recording clearly in mind. When tapes are the basic means of capturing the observations, ensuring the quality of the recorded data is crucial. Treating recording problems as annoying hassles that get in the way of the "real research" is a dangerous attitude with focus groups. The best research design and the most interesting questions matter little in the face of a blank tape or—even more maddening—one that sounds like a convention of chipmunks at the bottom of a swimming pool. In addition, all the effort and expense that went into the recruiting is wasted when a "technical problem" causes a loss of data.

Before going into the field, it is wise to get someone with technical experience to go over the recording setup (many colleges and universities have an audiovisual department that can provide this service). Once the recording equipment is set up at the site, it is absolutely vital to do a "live test." This consists of taping and replaying a brief statement on each recorder, even if it is just "testing, one, two, three." The specifics of actual recording setups depend on the nature of the field setting and the project budget, but two pieces of good advice are (a) pay equal attention to the quality of both the microphones and the tape recorders and (b) whenever possible, use two recording setups to provide a backup tape. In any event, it is always wise to bring along a hand-held recorder with fresh batteries in case of emergencies. Furthermore, if the session does not create a backup tape, then one should be made immediately to avoid losing the data after the fact.

Although videotaping is a tempting alternative to audiotaping, there is really very little to recommend it for social science research and there are several reasons to avoid it. A key difference between audiotaping and videotaping is the intrusiveness of the latter. Most people have few problems understanding the researcher's need for audiotaping to create a record of the discussions and then quickly settle into a discussion that ignores the microphones and tape recorders. By comparison, video setups that record full facial and nonverbal detail are quite complicated—requiring multiple cameras, supplemental lighting, and the absence of windows or other sources of backlighting. Even with all this equipment for video, it is important to remember that the actual analysis approach will most often be based on transcripts; simple video setups (e.g., single camera with built-in microphone) often have very low-quality audio and may require an external microphone along with a full audio setup as a source of backup data.

Given the greater invasion of privacy present with a video record, the researcher will need to give a clear and persuasive reason why this kind of information is of value to the project. Marketers do make considerable use of video because they frequently use edited "highlights" tapes as a major component of their ultimate report to the client. This is not a typical way to present social science research, but if it is a useful format for presenting the results of a particular project then it would be worthwhile to consider the expense and effort necessary to produce quality video recordings. One simple but expensive way to do videotaping is to rent a professional focus group facility.

One practical advantage that video does offer is the ability to determine who is speaking and, in conversations, who is speaking to whom. With audiotaping, this information is often not obvious from just listening to the tape. Therefore, research that requires a careful record of who was speaking to whom will require either video or an assistant who makes notes on this throughout the group. In the latter case, the transcript typist would then use the assistant's notes to identify each speaker. Counting on simple videotaping setups to provide much more information than this is probably overestimating the quality of what they capture. In particular, even high-quality video setups will not fully reproduce "group dynamics." As Marshall McLuhan noted, video has a tendency to cool things down. This is a large part of the reason why social scientists who use video to "capture nonverbals" are often disappointed with what they actually get. Although a video may remind the moderator of the emotions that were present around the table, it seldom conveys this same sense to someone who was not there during the original discussion.

A different issue is raised by the fact that marketing researchers typically use rooms that contain one-way mirrors, and renting such a facility means that a mirror will almost certainly be present. These setups allow marketing clients to observe a group and "get a feel" for the discussions, but it is difficult to imagine parallel needs for covert observation in the typical social science focus group. One possibility is when a project is extremely pressed for time and some members of the research team cannot wait for transcripts or summary analyses. There is little reason why one or two such observers could not sit in the room itself, however, especially if they are capable of acting in the role of assistants. The idea that observers should not be present in a room that already contains assistants, mirrors, microphones, and even video cameras is mostly just a matter of unquestioned tradition.

When supplementing the observations provided by focus groups, social scientists most often add the collection of questionnaires. Supplementing transcript data with questionnaires has both disadvantages and advantages. The largest disadvantage is that the two methods are mutually contaminating: Doing questionnaires first will direct the group discussion, whereas doing the group first may change the attitudes that appear in the questionnaires. Also, using questionnaires adds another layer of complexity; it is not a case of getting something for nothing. For example, it is more difficult to handle latecomers when using prequestionnaires; equivalently, with postquestionnaires, there will be difficulties with those who need to leave early.

Questionnaires do have some advantages, however. Getting at least a few background items can be quite useful. In particular, it can provide an accurate sense of who was in the group—for example, if there was an unintentionally limited range on social class. In any event, it is important to avoid survey-like interpretations of the questionnaire data, given the small size and nonrepresentativeness of the sample.

Regardless of whether the data collection includes questionnaires, there should be field notes from the moderator after each session. Experienced field-workers can either type or tape their own notes. If the moderator has little experience in social science or fieldwork, another member of the team can hold a "debriefing interview" with the moderator immediately after the session. Because these field notes involve interpretation, they are, properly speaking, part of the analysis rather than the data collection. Consequently, it is important to avoid reaching premature conclusions that can lead moderators to bias later groups in favor of confirming these expectations. Instead, note-taking should serve the goal of making emerging interpretations apparent so that the moderator can use this self-awareness either to limit unconscious attempts to confirm expectations or to make such efforts explicit.

Analysis and Reporting

LINKING ANALYSIS, REPORTING, AND RESEARCH DESIGN

I have joined together the topics of analysis and reporting because the type of analysis that is appropriate for a project is often highly dependent on the kind of report that the project will produce. Thinking about the nature of the report that the research should produce is an essential element in making decisions about how to analyze the data. When a project using focus groups fits the typical goals for qualitative research in the social sciences (e.g., to report the research in a peer-reviewed journal), then the general procedures for analyzing qualitative data in the social sciences will apply (e.g., Coffey & Atkinson, 1996; Miles & Huberman, 1994; Strauss & Corbin, 1990). There are, however, other uses of focus groups that call for rather different approaches to analysis and reporting.

When focus groups serve primarily as a preliminary, exploratory technique, the analysis and reporting of the data will typically be driven by the needs of the larger research project. For example, if the goal of the focus groups is to provide input into the design of an intervention program or to generate content for a survey questionnaire, then the analysis and reporting are likely to target the specific information needs of the larger project. Furthermore, because the report from preliminary focus groups will often be an oral briefing session or a brief technical document, the analysis is seldom as extensive as in a set of self-contained focus groups.

Between the limited analysis and reporting activities in preliminary focus groups and the more elaborate efforts associated with social science research projects, there is a set of intermediate cases in which the research typically has an applied purpose, such as an evaluation (Krueger, 1994). In applied research, the end result is often a detailed "final report" that must meet the needs to those who commissioned the project. Because many applied research projects investigate relatively predetermined research issues, they often use a more structured approach to gathering the data, which is matched by a similarly structured approach to analysis and reporting. In particular, when each group discussion covers more or less the same topics in more or less the same order, then the main business of the analysis and reporting will be to address these topics. Knodel (1993) describes the analysis of such data through a "grid" that systematically summarizes what each group said in response to each question. This approach is particularly useful when the research design separates the composition of the groups into "segments" because the use of a grid facilitates making and reporting comparisons across the different segments.

Raising issues such as the degree of structure in the interviews and the segmentation of the group composition points to the obvious influence that the research design has on the subsequent analysis of the data. For example, although using a more structured approach in collecting the data does not force the use of a group-by-question grid in the analysis, using a less structured approach certainly limits the value of this option. Similarly, choosing a research design that emphasizes cross-group comparisons (e.g., across different segments) automatically influences the nature of the analysis. Furthermore, a design that produces 30 groups presents analysis issues that are radically different from a design that produces 6 groups.

It is just as true, however, that analysis considerations will influence the original decisions about the research design. If a researcher lacks the analytic resources to make a systematic comparison of many groups across multiple segments, then it would be foolish (and even unethical) to collect unanalyzable data. Alternatively, if the ultimate goal is to report the findings in a peer-reviewed journal, then the research design must produce data that will satisfy the systematic and detailed analysis necessary for that goal. For example, no matter how detailed the analysis is from a single focus group, the analysis alone can never resolve the problem that the substantive content of the discussion may have been due to that one group's unique composition or dynamics. Thus, although analysis and reporting are the final stages in the research process, they are by no means left until the end of the project. As with other research methods in the social sciences, focus groups too can benefit from the classic advice that decisions about how to collect the data will depend on decisions about how to analyze and report the data.

CODING THE DATA

One unique issue that group interviews present for qualitative analysis concerns the unit of analysis in coding. Nearly all discussions of analysis issues in focus groups assert that the group, not the individual, must be the fundamental unit of analysis. The first edition of this book contained a similar admonition, but I have since broadened my thinking (Morgan, 1995). I now emphasize that the discussion in focus groups depends on both the individuals that make up the group and the dynamics of the group as a whole. In point of fact, most assertions that the group must be the unit of analysis are actually warnings about the dangers of using individuals as the unit of analysis. Although the influence of the group on individual participants is undeniable, this is a far cry from demonstrating that the group should then be the unit of analysis in focus group research.

The attempt to understand a group's activities as no more than the sum of the behaviors of its individual members amounts to the well-known fallacy of "psychological reductionism." The need to avoid psychological reductionism in analyzing focus groups is not, however, a warrant to engage in a form of "sociological reductionism," whereby the behaviors of individuals are treated as mere manifestations of an overarching group process. Instead, we must recognize not only that what individuals do in a group depends on the group context but also that what happens in any group depends on the individuals who make it up. In other words, neither the individual nor the group constitutes a separable "unit of analysis"; instead, our analytic efforts must seek a balance that acknowledges the interplay between these two "levels of analysis."

The practical importance of this issue is most apparent when it comes to coding the data from focus groups. The three most common ways of coding focus group transcripts are to note (a) all mentions of a given code, (b) whether each individual participant mentioned a given code, or (c) whether each group's discussion contained a given code. In practice, these three strategies are nested within each other because coding all mentions of a topic will also determine whether that topic was mentioned by a specific individual or in a particular group. Consequently, the recent versions of several computer programs for qualitative analysis (e.g., Richards & Richards, 1995; Seidel, Freise, & Leonard, 1995) can readily generate reports about which groups and which participants have which portions of their text associated with any given code. Coding that is truly at the group level, however, often requires judgments that go beyond aggregating codes at the individual level (see Gamson, 1992, for one approach to generating codes at the group level).

Other coding concerns are more familiar. As with other forms of qualitative data, the nature of coding in focus groups differs between approaches that apply a priori "templates" to the coding versus those that produce the codes through a more emergent encounter with the data themselves (Crabtree & Miller, 1992). Whether the goal is to fine-tune an existing coding template or to create a new set of codes, it helps to begin with a detailed examination of one or two groups before applying the resulting codes to the remainder of the groups. A useful variant on this strategy is to have one person examine one set of transcripts while another does a similar preliminary analysis on a different set of discussions; this allows for two processes of discovery in the material.

Once the codes exist in the data, the question of whether to count them is as controversial with focus groups as it is with other forms of qualitative data. One specific argument against using numbers in focus groups is that such data violate the assumption of independence that is necessary for many statistical analyses. The mere collection of observations in groups, however, does not necessarily violate statistical laws; instead, it requires proper allowances for the fact that the data are grouped. Experimental designs based on "nested data" are a classic approach to this issue. "Multilevel analysis" (DiPrete & Forrestal, 1994) has provided techniques for simultaneously analyzing individual-level and group-level aspects of such data. Those whose research questions require statistical tests on data from focus groups would be well-advised to consult with an expert in the analysis of "grouped data" prior to entering the field.

I believe that some quantitative uses of coding are both obvious and useful in analyzing transcripts from focus groups (Morgan, 1993c). In my own work, I often present simple counts of codes without performing any statistical tests (e.g., Morgan & March 1992; Morgan & Zhao, 1993). Sophisticated debates about independent observations, random sampling, and so on do not apply to using descriptive statistics to summarize the content of focus groups. Descriptive counting is especially useful in research projects that compare distinctively different groups to determine how often various topics are mentioned in the different types of groups; for example, Shively (1992) has used comparisons between ethnic groups. The real argument here is not over whether qualitative researchers want to characterize differences between groups but whether numerical characterizations of those differences add anything to our understanding.

The debate about using numbers in interpreting focus groups is, to a large extent, due to a failure to distinguish between the qualitative collection of data and the qualitative analysis of those data. Focus groups will always remain a qualitative technique for generating data, regardless of how the data are handled. When it comes to analyzing focus groups, some researchers will not feel comfortable answering their research questions with numbers, whereas others will not feel comfortable without them. Those who can answer their research questions without counting codes should feel well justified in doing so—no appeals to imagined problems with statistical independence or random sampling are necessary. Furthermore, those who argue for the advantages of a qualitative analysis of qualitative data should feel secure enough in their own approach to pursue it without bothering to attack the additional possibility of doing quantitative analyses on the same data.

INTERPRETING THE DATA

Interpreting the data from focus groups requires distinguishing between what participants find interesting and what they find important. When participants discuss a topic at length, this is a good indication that they find it interesting, but that is not the same as saying that they think it is important. Alternatively, a brief discussion of a topic may indicate that participants find it uninteresting and not unimportant. For example, in our study of perceptions of heart attack risk factors (Morgan & Spanish, 1985), we found that the participants spent a great deal of time discussing stress but very little time discussing cigarette smoking. Although this is good evidence that the participants found stress to be a more interesting topic than smoking, it certainly does not imply that they thought stress was a more important cause of heart attacks than smoking.

The most basic method for determining what the participants think is important is to ask them! Many interview guides thus anticipate the ultimate analysis and interpretation of the data by asking a final question that has the participants state what they think the most important elements of the discussion have been. In projects in which the central goal is to determine the importance of different topics, these topics may be sorted into a list that the participants rate or rank. Regardless of the specific technique, the fundamental message here is that learning what the participants think is important should be built into the data collection itself—not left to the analyst's post hoc speculation.

Quite often, interpreting focus group data comes down to a question of which topics should receive the most emphasis in the eventual report. There are three basic factors that influence how much emphasis a given topic should receive: how many groups mentioned the topic, how many people within each of these groups mentioned the topic, and how much energy and enthusiasm the topic generated among the participants. The best evidence that a topic is worth emphasizing comes from a combination of all three of these factors that is known as "group-to-group validation." For any specific topic, group-to-group validation means that whenever a topic comes up, it generates a consistent level of energy among a consistent proportion of the participants across nearly all the groups. For example, a project might produce group-to-group validation that a specific topic consistently produces either excitement or boredom, either consensus or controversy, and so on. Furthermore, some projects produce a larger sense of group-to-group validation when nearly all of the groups share similar reactions across nearly all the topics that they discuss.

The concept of group-to-group validation calls attention to the fact that nearly all analyses of focus groups concentrate on the manifest content of the group discussions. In contrast, there has been little attention to the microdynamics of the interaction process in focus groups (for discussions of these issues, see Agar & MacDonald, 1995; Saferstein, 1995). To be sure, moderators do pay attention to the nonverbal aspects of group interaction, but this is nothing like the careful attention to turn-taking, eye contact, pauses in interaction, patterns of speech, and so on that could go into an analysis of these conversations. The present discussion has thus emphasized the substantive content of focus groups, although future efforts to explore other dimensions of the interaction in focus groups would be quite welcome.

REPORTING

The similarity between focus groups and other qualitative methods is most apparent when it comes to reporting the results of the research. As with other qualitative means of data collection, there are no hard and fast rules when it comes to reporting results. In large part, the format will reflect earlier decisions. According to Becker (1986), by the time the social scientist sits down to write, most of the big choices about how to portray the research have already been made during the course of the research itself. With focus groups, these choices include whether the research was exploratory or hypothesis testing, whether the level of moderator involvement was intended to produce structured or unstructured discussions, and whether the analyses relied on either the counting of codes or more interpretive summaries of the data.

Writing the actual report of the results requires a balance between the direct quotation of the participants and the summarization of their discussions. Too many quotations give the report a chaotic, stream-of-consciousness flavor. Too much summarization is not only dry but also deprives the reader of even the indirect contact with participants that their verbatim statements provide. Focus groups are no different from other qualitative methods in this regard: There is a perpetual tension between the richness of the data and the remoteness of the reader from the sources of the data. Reducing this remoteness is often the goal of qualitative research, but this is best done through a report that first separates the topics that are more important from those that are less important and then concentrates on a thorough portrayal of only what is most important. Thus, the goal of connecting the reader and the original participants through "well-chosen" quotations requires a match between the importance of the topic and vividness of the example.

Summing Up

Much of the material in this and the previous chapter has, of necessity, concentrated on technical matters that affect choices between alternate versions of the focus group technique. Like any truly useful method of data collection, focus groups have the flexibility to provide researchers with a range of options to respond to a variety of circumstances. Appropriate choices among these options require an understanding of the more technical aspects of focus groups. If this presentation has met its goal, the reader will have not only a mastery of the technical aspects of focus groups but also a sense of why the issues raised here are critical concerns in planning, conducting, and analyzing focus group research.

Although there is an undeniable need to understand the range of options that focus groups provide, it is also important not to lose track of the larger issues that influence choices among these options. In particular, the theme that practical decisions depend on larger research goals has appeared several times throughout this discussion. For example, research that explores previously uncharted territory is likely to require a different format from research that decides among well-established competing hypotheses. Making such decisions requires a degree of mastery over the technical aspects of focus groups, but that mastery is not an end in itself. Ultimately, the choices that are made depend on the goals that must be served.

6. ADDITIONAL POSSIBILITIES

The future development of focus groups offers many opportunities thanks to the relative newness of the technique. What distinguishes most of the research designs that I present in this chapter is the fact that they involve systematic variations across groups. That systematic attention to alternatives is the key to research design with focus groups.

In addition to what I present here, other "additional possibilities" for focus group research have already arisen in earlier chapters. For example, the final section of Chapter 5 noted that the microprocesses associated with the interaction in focus groups remain virtually unexplored. Moreover, the comparisons between group and individual interviews presented in Chapters 2 and 3 contained several suggestions for comparing these two approaches to collecting qualitative data. The present emphasis on additional possibilities is thus a continuation of, rather than a departure from, the themes in the previous chapters. A word of warning is in order, however. Many of the ideas in this chapter remain untried, and others may have been used only once or twice. Consequently, what follows is best approached as a set of suggestions for extending the kinds of research that we do with focus groups.

Factors That Affect the Nature of the Discussion

At a conference at which social science researchers considered "Future Directions for Focus Groups" (Morgan, 1993b), we advocated doing more research on how what we do in focus groups is linked with the nature of the data that we collect. One of the most obvious factors that affect what we learn from focus groups is the set of questions that guide the discussion. A research program based on varying the questions in the groups is a straightforward option. A concrete example would be to investigate the strengths and weakness of the commonly used funnel design: In what circumstances is it most useful to begin with questions about more general issues and progressively narrow in on the topics that interest the researcher most? When would researchers do better to use an alternative to this format?

An example of how research might address alternatives in asking questions comes from the project we did on perceptions of heart attacks (Morgan & Spanish, 1985). Because we were working with healthy people in their thirties and forties who typically had had little involvement with the topic of heart attacks, we used an "inverted funnel" that worked from more specific to more general questions. First, we asked each participant to share a story about a person that they knew who had had a heart attack. Then, we asked the participants to compare their stories, and to tell us more stories, as part of a discussion of "Who has heart attacks and why?" Finally, we asked them to connect what they had been saying to the broad topic of "What causes and what prevents heart attacks?" Although that approach worked very well for this particular project, we do not know whether it worked better than a classic funnel approach. We also do not know if those two different approaches would have led to rather different discussions of the same underlying topic. Had we conducted some groups that used the classic funnel and compared them to the ones that used an inverted funnel, we would be able to speak to this issue.

Another straightforward research topic on questioning concerns the amount of structure that the questions impose on the discussion. One example would be a project that compared the use of topic guides versus questioning routes as formats for asking the questions. Topic guides simply list the issues to be covered during the discussion and are often described as producing a less structured, more free-flowing conversation than questioning routes that organize the interview around a specific set of questions (Krueger, 1994). Rather than making this blanket generalization, it would be useful to know when a particular set of participants discussing a particular topic would benefit from one approach rather than the other. We could investigate that issue by conducting studies that compared question routes and topic guides across different groups within the same research project.

Beyond the questions, another obvious factor that affects the nature of the data in focus groups is the moderator. McDonald (1993) presents an interesting approach to making comparisons among moderators by using archival data. By comparing tapes, transcripts, and reports from different moderators who had worked on a large number of marketing projects, he concluded that different styles of moderating did indeed produce different results. Certainly the same general conclusion would apply to moderators from the social sciences as well, but what dimensions should we consider either when comparing our moderating styles or when assessing how they affect our data? Fortunately, the rapidly growing body of focus group research in the social sciences may create the opportunity to address such issues using archival data.

Group size provides a final example of research on factors that affect the nature of focus group data. Even within the "typical" size range of 6 to 10 participants, there is an intuitive feeling that a group of 6 would be too small for some topics and a group of 10 too large for others. I am not aware, however, of any systematic attempt to document how differences in topics match up with differences in preferred group size. If we believe that smaller groups are especially valuable for topics that are "sensitive" or that generate high levels of participant involvement, then this should be easy to demonstrate by comparing how smaller versus larger groups discuss such topics. A parallel design also applies, of course, to the belief that larger groups are more valuable for topics that generate low levels of participant involvement.

Effects of Group Composition

Technically speaking, varying group composition should be grouped together with other factors that affect the nature of the data. I have separated out variations in group composition because of the substantial amount of work that already exists in this area. A good example is Knodel, et al.'s, and Pramualratana's (1984) study of different generations in Thailand to compare their views on family size and family planning. As it happens, Knodel et al. found broad agreement between the two generations, with both believing that small family sizes were desirable for members of the younger generation. The key point, however, is that this similarity could not have been demonstrated without a systematic variation in the composition of the groups.

A somewhat different reason for varying group composition is to determine whether either what people say or the way they say it varies with the context of the group. An example would extend Wight's (1994) finding that adolescent males give different data in individual versus peer-group interviews: How would their self-portrayals differ between same-sex and mixed-sex groups? Varying the composition of focus groups thus provides an extremely useful way to pursue the "context-dependent" nature of qualitative data.

Another way to investigate the effects of group composition is through a "mix-and-match" design in which some groups mix together different categories of participants, whereas other groups match the participants to assure homogeneity. Templeton (1994) provides a marketing example of the differences that occur in mixed versus matched groups. She first conducted a set of groups on hair coloring that combined women who did and did not dye their hair. The result was the kind of hostility that is often warned against in mixed groups, with the women who did not dye their hair expressing a great deal of anger toward advertising that suggested that gray hair was not attractive to men. When women who did not dye their hair talked among themselves in a homogeneous group, however, they expressed considerably more self-doubt about their choice to keep their hair gray. For a social science example of a mix-and-match design, consider the question of whether to interview husbands and wives together. Inviting a set of husband-wife couples to a focus group creates the possibility of conducting not only groups in which both halves of a couple participate together but also homogeneous groups that separate men and women or mixed groups of men and women that are divided so that no one participates in the same group as his or her spouse. These kinds of comparisons would help to get at issues of gender differences as well as the inhibiting or releasing effect of having a spouse present.

A final example of mixing group composition involves research in which the goal is to understand how different perspectives operate in the same setting. As a first step, this might involve conducting separate focus groups within each of the relevant categories. Although this would produce a tentative understanding of the ways that participants from various perspectives both overlap and diverge, it would tell us little about the dynamics of interaction between them. That would require a further set of mixed groups. This progression from matched groups to mixed groups might well uncover statements that can be said in homogeneous groups but not in mixed company. Alternatively, new statements could appear in a mixed discussion that would not come up among those who all share the same perspective. Either way, the results could be illuminating.

Changes in Groups Over Time

The idea of using an earlier set of groups as the basis for a later set of groups points to research designs that use an over-time dimension. Such changes over time are inherent in any qualitative design that emphasizes "emergence," in which future research activities are explicitly contingent on what is learned through an ongoing encounter with the data. In addition, it is also possible to plan in advance for changes in the research design such as a switch from an initial set of homogeneous groups to a subsequent set of mixed groups.

A different kind of variation over time occurs when the same participants are brought back for more than one group. In this case, the comparison is between the earlier and later sessions. The most basic version of this design has the same groups meeting together several times. As the group members get to know each other, a sense of rapport is built, individual biographies and preferences are learned, and a sense of shared history develops. These "longitudinal groups" thus raise a variety of issues that do not occur in the typical "one-shot" use of focus groups.

This increasing familiarity implies that the later groups in a longitudinal sequence will require less in the way of structured guides or explicit self-management techniques because these groups are likely to take on a life of their own. When the groups expect to meet again, there is likely to be a heightened awareness of the research topic throughout this interim period. This awareness can be built into the research design, including the possibility of giving "assignments" at the end of one session that will serve as the starting point for the next discussion (e.g., "Between now and the next time, I'd like you each to pay particular attention to anything that makes you think about _____. That way, we can find out more about when this whole issue comes up in your day-to-day lives.").

Another kind of multistage group can be created in designs that mix together participants from several different earlier groups in what can be termed "second-order" groups. Mixing participants from previous groups naturally leads to a comparison of the discussions in the several original groups; therefore, it may be wise to include no more than one member from each of the prior discussions. We recruited such a second-order group from the original participants in our focus groups on heart attack risk factors (Morgan & Spanish, 1985). In that follow-up group, we first asked each person to provide a brief summary of what was discussed in his or her group and then left the rest of the discussion unstructured. What we learned was that the returning students who served as our participants in this project were more interested in stress than in heart attacks, and that our preferred topic was almost submerged in a general discussion of stress and coping. This led us to explore the possibilities of a new research project based on the exploration of "folk beliefs" about stress.

As this example shows, running later, second-order groups in a relatively unstructured fashion allows the researcher to discover which topics from the earlier groups continue to interest the participants. It could thus be useful to run second-order groups with low moderator involvement after a first set of highly structured groups as a way to encounter differences between the participants' perspective and the researcher's. Also, there is no reason to stop at second-order groups: Provided that sufficient participants were available, participants from second-order groups could be mixed together to form third-order groups, and so on.

Goldman (1962) describes yet another form of multistage group based on mixing prior participants with new participants. In his study, an initial group of participants met together several times to discuss their feelings about some radically new designs for appliances; over the course of their several discussions, the initially negative reactions of these participants became substantially more positive. To see whether this enthusiasm was transferable, Goldman then asked the continuing participants to meet with a set of people who had never seen the new designs before. In this mixed group, the continuing participants had difficulty explaining their enthusiasm to the new participants, which led the continuing participants to revert to their earlier skepticism. Consequently, the redesign project was dropped. Goldman suggests that this approach to focus groups comes closer to duplicating interaction in natural contexts, in which opinions must first be formed and then communicated and defended.

A final set of over-time possibilities consists of using a sequential set of groups to "track" changes. Here, there is no attempt to bring back the participants from previous groups. Instead, this design recruits successive groups from similar sources while using similar questions in each interview. Comparing the discussions across the set of groups provides information about changes and trends. Variations on this basic design are most common in the study of public opinion (Delli Carpini & Williams, 1994). One obvious use of focus groups in tracking public opinion is to monitor changes in voters' responses to candidates during an election campaign, but a similar research design could also be used to pursue almost any social issue or behavior pattern that was subject to change over time.

Changes Within Groups

The most obvious kind of change that focus groups might produce results from participating in the group itself. The basic idea that group discussions can produce attitude change goes back to Kurt Lewin and beyond. For example, for the focus groups on heart attack risk factors (Morgan & Spanish, 1985), we asked participants to complete pre- and postquestionnaires that measured whether the participants felt that most individuals were or were not responsible for causing their own heart attacks. Sussman et al. (1991) also used a "pre-post" design to determine whether participating in focus groups would change teenagers' opinions about which strategies would promote smoking cessation. A common variant on this approach is to determine how the group discussion (and questionnaire ratings) changes following the introduction of "stimulus material," such as films and videotapes, storyboard summaries, mock-ups of brochures, or brief textual descriptions.

A different approach to studying the effects of focus groups comes from studies that use "postgroup questionnaires" to assess participants' responses to the group itself. For example, Pies (1993) studied earlier users of a new form of birth control and, at the end of the group, asked them to complete a brief survey about both their level of comfort during the discussion and whether there were some things that they had not been willing to say in the group (and if so, what those were). This kind of postgroup questionnaire can provide valuable information about how the group setting affects the reactions of different categories of participants to various aspects of the discussion. Such questionnaires could also help detect any ethical concerns or sources of stress that were not obvious in the group setting. This same approach could also be extended to include follow-up individual interviews, either in person or by phone, to find out more about participants' reaction to participating in a focus group.

Summing Up

The additional possibilities in this chapter are a good demonstration of the range of uses for focus groups. This list is far from exhaustive, however. At this point, we may only have scratched the surface with regard to the possible ways of doing focus group research. There is, however, nothing inherently superior about a complex or innovative research design. Ultimately, what will determine the value of these designs is whether they can answer our research questions in ways that go beyond what we could accomplish with simpler or tried-and-true approaches.

7. CONCLUSIONS

The conclusions to the first edition of this book began by noting: "The contribution of focus groups to social science research is, at present, more potential than real." Today, the situation is quite different. The past decade has produced a steady increase in social scientists' use of focus groups, and there is a widespread consensus that focus groups are a valuable technique for collecting qualitative data.

If we have reached the point where focus groups are widely accepted, what is the next step? I believe that those of us who work with focus groups now face two different challenges. First, we must build on the lessons that we have learned so that we can share the existing state of the art. Second, we must create new approaches to focus groups so that we can advance the state of the art.

SHARING THE EXISTING STATE OF THE ART

Since social scientists rediscovered focus groups in the early 1980s, we have worked hard to adapt the technique to our purposes. We have learned a great deal about how to do focus groups, and many of the lessons that we have learned will continue to be of value. As new practitioners join our ranks, we need to share what we have learned.

One of the lessons that I have tried to convey throughout this book is the importance of thinking about focus groups in terms of research design. Put another way, it is important to understand all the elements that go into a focus group research project. Some people still think of focus groups solely in terms of the specific skills that go into moderating a group discussion. In reality, the success of the project as a whole depends on a combination of thoughtfully defining the research goals, systematically deciding what questions need to be asked, carefully determining who will participate in the groups and how to recruit them, and thoroughly analyzing the data in addition to skillfully moderating the groups.

In the course of describing these design issues, I have offered a great many suggestions about how to do (and not to do) focus groups. Although I certainly believe in the value of sharing this summary of the current state of the art, I am also concerned about the dangers of relying too heavily on this body of "received wisdom." I am particularly concerned that future users of focus groups will justify their research designs by simply citing texts such as this one rather than carefully thinking through the decisions that need to be made.

One way out of this dilemma is to insist that there is no "one right way" to do focus groups. Instead, there are a great many choices that must be made. To judge the quality of research using focus groups, we must assess the soundness of the decisions that the researcher has made. An active awareness of the current state of the art is thus necessary for doing high-quality work with focus groups. Parroting the received wisdom is not sufficient evidence that the work was done well.

ADVANCING THE STATE OF THE ART

Relying on received wisdom about how to use focus groups also carries the danger of cutting short the future development of the method. At this point, most of our knowledge about focus groups still comes from "learning by doing." There is thus a clear value in further experimentation with focus groups because trying new experiments will help us learn about the range of possibilities that we could be incorporating. As Chapter 6 on additional possibilities demonstrates, I believe that innovative approaches to focus groups will promote the growth of our field. In addition, we can take a further step to advance the state of our art by conducting self-conscious methodological research on focus groups.

One of the most distinctive contributions that social scientists could make to focus groups would be to undertake a systematic program of research on this method. Indeed, the discussion of "future directions" (Morgan, 1993b) that we conducted among social scientists who were using focus groups highlighted the need for more methodological research. That group believed that doing research on focus groups would not only provide us with evidence for the value of current practices but also set a standard for testing new techniques.

One useful strategy for doing research on focus groups is to include methodological components in ongoing research. This essentially amounts to varying the research procedures across groups to find out what difference it makes to do experiments one way rather than another. Using new approaches along with more traditional procedures combines the methodological advantage of creating a head-to-head comparison with the practical advantage of not relying solely on unproven techniques. This combination is especially useful when testing new techniques.

In our discussion of future directions, we also advocated getting a wider array of disciplines involved in doing focus groups. Our hope was to re-create the innovations that occurred when the first wave of social scientists who did focus groups questioned the wisdom that we received. By bringing in a new set of social science researchers from other disciplines, we would set the stage for questioning our own received wisdom. Fortunately, there is evidence that an increasing range of social science disciplines are using focus groups (Morgan, 1996); therefore, only time will tell if this does indeed broaden the range of practices.

In looking forward to a future generation of focus group researchers, from both other disciplines and within our own ranks, I believe that we need to offer them two things. First, we need to provide clear statements about what our procedures are and why we have been doing focus groups this way—that is, we need to share the current state of the art. Second, we need to give them a mandate to produce new and better ways to do focus groups—that is, we need to advance the state of the art.

In presenting my own summary of both the present and the future of focus groups, I have done my best not to overstate the case. There are always short-term advantages to extravagant claims, if only to overcome the inertia that is associated with getting someone to learn a new technique. My preference, however, is to avoid the long-run disappointment that comes from creating unrealistic expectations.

Ultimately, focus groups will be judged against one unavoidable criterion: Do they help us reach our research goals? At a minimum, any new method must offer researchers an increased sense that they can answer their existing research questions. New methods are especially appealing, however, when they also lead us to ask new or better questions. Thus, the appeal of focus groups as an addition to the existing range of qualitative techniques arises from their ability both to address existing research questions and to generate new ideas about how to do qualitative research.

REFERENCES

Agar, M. H. (1986). *Speaking of ethnography* (Sage University Paper, Qualitative Research Methods series, Vol. 2). Beverly Hills, CA: Sage.

Agar, M. H., & MacDonald, J. (1995). Focus groups and ethnography. *Human Organization, 54,* 78-86.

Andreason, A. (1995). *Marketing social change: Changing behaviors to promote health, social development, and the environment.* San Francisco: Jossey-Bass.

Axelrod, M. D. (1975). Marketers get an eyeful when focus groups expose products, ideas, images, and copy, etc. to consumers. *Marketing News, 8,* 6-7.

Basch, C. E. (1987). Focus group interview: An underutilized research technique for improving theory and practice in health education. *Health Education Quarterly, 14,* 411-448.

Bauman, L. J., & Adair, E. G. (1992). The use of ethnographic interviewing to inform questionnaire construction. *Health Education Quarterly, 19,* 19-24.

Becker, H. S. (1958). Problems of inference and proof in participant observation. *American Sociological Review, 23,* 652-660.

Becker, H. S. (1986). *Writing for social scientists.* Chicago: University of Chicago Press.

Becker, H. S., & Greer, B. (1957). Participant observation and interviewing: A comparison. *Human Organization, 16,* 28-32.

Berry, W. D., & Feldman, S. (1985). *Multiple regression in practice.* Beverly Hills, CA: Sage.

Bogardus, E. S. (1926). The group interview. *Journal of Applied Sociology, 10,* 372-382.

Bryant, C. A. (1990). The use of focus groups in program development. *National Association of Practicing Anthropologists Bulletin, 39,* 1-4.

Bryman, A. (1988). *Quality and quantity in social research.* New York: Routledge.

Calder, B. J. (1977). Focus groups and the nature of qualitative marketing research. *Journal of Marketing Research, 14,* 353-364.

Carey, M. A. (1995). Issues and applications of focus groups: Introduction. *Journal of Qualitative Health Research, 5,* 413.

Coffey, A., & Atkinson, P. (1996). *Making sense of qualitative data: Complementary strategies.* Thousand Oaks, CA: Sage.

Converse, J. M., & Presser, S. (1986). *Survey questions: Handcrafting the standardized questionnaire* (Sage University Paper, Quantitative Research Methods series, Vol. 63). Beverly Hills, CA: Sage.

Crabtree, B. F., & Miller, W. L. (1992). A template approach to codebook analysis: Developing and using codebooks. In B. F. Crabtree & W. L. Miller (Eds.), *Doing qualitative research in primary care: Multiple strategies* (pp. 93-109). Newbury Park, CA: Sage.

Crabtree, B. F., Yanoshik, M. K., Miller, W. L., & O'Connor, P. J. (1993). Selecting individual or group interviews. In D. L. Morgan (Ed.), *Successful focus groups: Advancing the state of the art* (pp. 137-154). Newbury Park, CA: Sage.

Delli Carpini, M. X., & Williams, B. (1994). The method is the message: Focus groups as a method of social, psychological, and political inquiry. *Research in Micropolitics, 4,* 57-85.

DiPrete, T. A., & Forrestal, J. D. (1994). Multilevel models: Methods and substance. In J. Hagan & K. S. Cook (Eds.), *Annual review of sociology* (Vol. 20, pp. 331-357). Palo Alto, CA: Annual Reviews.

Duncan, M. T., & Morgan, D. L. (1994). Sharing the caring: Family caregivers' views of their relationships with nursing home staff. *The Gerontologist, 34,* 235-244.

Fern, E. F. (1982). The use of focus groups for idea generation: The effects of group size, acquaintanceship, and moderator on response quantity and quality. *Journal of Marketing Research, 19,* 1-13.

Folch-Lyon, E., de la Macorra, L., & Schearer, S. B. (1981). Focus group and survey research on family planning in Mexico. *Studies in Family Planning, 12,* 409-432.

Frey, J. H., & Fontana, A. (1989). The group interview in social research. *Social Science Journal, 28,* 175-187. (Also pp. 3-19 in Morgan, 1993a)

Fuller, T. D., Edwards, J. N., Vorakitphokatorn, S., & Sermsri, S. (1993). Using focus groups to adapt survey instruments to new populations: Experience from a developing country. In D. L. Morgan (Ed.), *Successful focus groups: Advancing the state of the art* (pp. 89-104). Newbury Park, CA: Sage.

Gamson, W. A. (1992). *Talking politics.* New York: Cambridge University Press.

Glaser, B. G., & Strauss, A. L. (1967). *The discovery of grounded theory.* Chicago: Aldine.

Goldman, A. E. (1962). The group depth interview. *Journal of Marketing, 26,* 61-68.

Goldman, A. E., & McDonald, S. S. (1987). *The group depth interview: Principles and practice.* Englewood Cliffs, NJ: Prentice Hall.

Greenbaum, T. L. (1993). *The practical handbook and guide to focus group research* (Rev. ed.). Lexington, MA: Lexington Books.

Gubrium, J. F. (1987). *Oldtimers and Alzheimer's: The descriptive organization of senility.* Greenwich, CT: JAI.

Hayes, T. J., & Tatham, C. B. (1989). *Focus group interviews: A reader* (2nd ed.). Chicago: American Marketing Association.

Hochschild, A. R. (1983). *The managed heart: Commercialization of human feeling.* Berkeley: University of California Press.

Hughes, D., & DuMont, K. (1993). Using focus groups to facilitate culturally anchored research. *American Journal of Community Psychology, 21,* 775-806.

Ingersoll, F., & Ingersoll, J. (1987). Both a borrower and a lender be: Ethnography, oral history, grounded theory. *Oral History Review, 15,* 81-102.

Irwin, J. (1970). *The felon.* Englewood Cliffs, NJ: Prentice Hall.

Janis, I. L. (1982). *Groupthink* (2nd ed.). Boston: Houghton Mifflin.

Jarrett, R. L. (1993). Focus group interviewing with low-income, minority populations: A research experience. In D. L. Morgan (Ed.), *Successful focus groups: Advancing the state of the art* (pp. 184-201). Newbury Park, CA: Sage.

Jarrett, R. L. (1994). Living poor: Family life among single parent, African-American women. *Social Problems, 41,* 30-49.

Joseph, J. G., Emmons, C.-A., Kessler, R. C., Wortman, C. B., O'Brien, K. J., Hocker, W. T., & Schaefer, C. (1984). Coping with the threat of AIDS: An approach to psychosocial assessment. *American Psychologist, 39,* 1297-1302.

Khan, M. E., & Manderson, L. (1992). Focus groups in tropical diseases research. *Health Policy and Planning, 7,* 56-66.

Kirk, J., & Miller, M. L. (1986). *Reliability and validity of qualitative research* (Sage University Paper, Qualitative Research Methods series, Vol. 1). Beverly Hills, CA: Sage.

Kitzinger, J. (1994a). The methodology of focus groups: The importance of interaction between research participants. *Sociology of Health and Illness, 16,* 103-121.

Kitzinger, J. (1994b). Focus groups: Method or madness. In M. Boulton (Ed.), *Challenge and innovation: Methodological advances in social research on HIV/AIDS* (pp. 159-175). New York: Taylor & Francis.

Knodel, J. (1993). The design and analysis of focus group studies: A practical approach. In D. L. Morgan (Ed.), *Successful focus groups: Advancing the state of the art* (pp. 35-50). Newbury Park, CA: Sage.

Knodel, J. (1995). Focus groups as a method for cross-cultural research in social gerontology. *Journal of Cross-Cultural Gerontology, 10,* 7-20.

Knodel, J., Chamratrithirong, A., & Debavalya, N. (1987). *Thailand's reproductive revolution: Rapid fertility decline in a Third-World setting.* Madison: University of Wisconsin Press.

Knodel, J., Havanon, N., & Pramualratana, A. (1984). Fertility transition in Thailand: A qualitative analysis. *Population and Development Review, 10,* 297-328.

Krueger, R. A. (1993). Quality control in focus group research. In D. L. Morgan (Ed.), *Successful focus groups: Advancing the state of the art* (pp. 65-88). Newbury Park, CA: Sage.

Krueger, R. A. (1994). *Focus groups: A practical guide for applied research* (2nd ed.). Thousand Oaks, CA: Sage.

Laurie, H., & Sullivan, O. (1991). Combining qualitative and quantitative data in the longitudinal study of household allocations. *Sociological Review, 39,* 113-130.

Lazarsfeld, P. F. (1972). *Qualitative analysis: Historical and critical essays.* Boston: Allyn & Bacon.

Lunt, P., & Livingstone, S. (1996). Rethinking focus groups in media and communication. *Journal of Communication, 46,* 79-98.

Marshall, C., & Rossman, G. B. (1995). *Designing qualitative research* (2nd ed.). Thousand Oaks, CA: Sage.

McDonald, W. J. (1993). Focus group research dynamics and reporting: An examination of research objectives and moderator influences. *Journal of the Academy of Marketing Science, 21,* 161-168.

McQuarrie, E. F. (1996). *The market research toolbox: A concise guide for beginners.* Thousand Oaks, CA: Sage.

Merton, R. K., Fiske, M., & Kendall, P. L. (1990). *The focused interview* (2nd ed.). New York: Free Press.

Merton, R. K., & Kendall, P. L. (1946). The focussed interview. *American Journal of Sociology, 51,* 541-557.

Merton, R. K., Reader, G. G., & Kendall, P. L. (1957). *The student physician.* Cambridge, MA: Harvard University Press.

Miles, M. B., & Huberman, A. M. (1994). *Qualitative data analysis* (2nd ed.). Thousand Oaks, CA: Sage.

Morgan, D. L. (1986). Personal relationships as an interface between social networks and social cognitions. *Journal of Social and Personal Relationships, 3,* 403-442.

Morgan, D. L. (1989). Adjusting to widowhood: Do social networks really make it easier? *The Gerontologist, 29,* 101-107.

Morgan, D. L. (1992a). Designing focus group research. In M. Stewart, F. Tudiver, M. J. Bass, E. V. Dunn, & P. G. Norton (Eds.), *Tools for primary care research* (pp. 194-208). Newbury Park, CA: Sage.

Morgan, D. L. (1992b). Doctor caregiver relationships: An exploration using focus groups. In B. F. Crabtree & W. L. Miller (Eds.), *Doing qualitative research in primary care: Multiple strategies* (pp. 205-230). Newbury Park, CA: Sage.

Morgan, D. L. (Ed.). (1993a). *Successful focus groups: Advancing the state of the art.* Newbury Park, CA: Sage.

Morgan, D. L. (1993b). Future directions for focus groups. In D. L. Morgan (Ed.), *Successful focus groups: Advancing the state of the art* (pp. 225-244). Newbury Park, CA: Sage.

Morgan, D. L. (1993c). Qualitative content analysis: A guide to paths not taken. *Qualitative Health Research, 2,* 112-121.

Morgan, D. L. (1995). Why things (sometimes) go wrong in focus groups. *Qualitative Health Research, 5,* 515-522.

Morgan, D. L. (1996). Focus groups. In J. Hagan & K. S. Cook (Eds.), *Annual review of sociology* (Vol. 22, pp. 129-152). Palo Alto, CA: Annual Reviews.

Morgan, D. L., & Krueger, R. A. (1993). When to use focus groups and why. In D. L. Morgan (Ed.), *Successful focus groups: Advancing the state of the art* (pp. 3-19). Newbury Park, CA: Sage.

Morgan, D. L., & March, S. J. (1992). The impact of life events on networks of personal relationships: A comparison of widowhood and caring for a spouse with Alzheimer's disease. *Journal of Social and Personal Relationships, 9,* 563-584.

Morgan, D. L., & Spanish, M. T. (1984). Focus groups: A new tool for qualitative research. *Qualitative Sociology, 7,* 253-270.

Morgan, D. L., & Spanish, M. T. (1985). Social interaction and the cognitive organisation of health-relevant behavior. *Sociology of Health and Illness, 7,* 401-422.

Morgan, D. L., & Zhao, P. Z. (1993). The doctor-caregiver relationship: Managing the care of family members with Alzheimer's disease. *Qualitative Health Research, 3,* 133-164.

O'Brien, K. J. (1993). Using focus groups to develop health surveys: An example from research on social relationships and AIDS-preventive behavior. *Health Education Quarterly, 20,* 361-372. (Also pp. 105-117 in Morgan, 1993a)

Patton, M. Q. (1990). *Qualitative evaluation and research methods* (2nd ed.). Newbury Park, CA: Sage.

Pies, C. (1993). *Controversies in context: Ethics, values, and policies concerning NOR-PLANT.* Unpublished doctoral dissertation, University of California, Berkeley.

Pramualratana, A., Havanon, N., & Knodel, J. (1985). Exploring the normative age at marriage in Thailand: An example from focus group research. *Journal of Marriage and the Family, 47,* 203-210.

Punch, M. (1986). *Politics and ethics of fieldwork* (Sage University Paper, Qualitative Research Methods series, Vol. 3). Beverly Hills, CA: Sage.

Richards, T. J., & Richards, L. (1995). *User's guide for QSR NUD•IST.* Melbourne, Australia: Qualitative Solutions and Research.

Rogers, E. M. (1994). *A history of communication study: A biographical approach.* New York: Free Press.

Rossi, P. H., Wright, J. D., & Anderson, A. B. (Eds.). (1983). *Handbook of survey research.* New York: Academic Press.

Saferstein, B. (1995). *Focusing opinions: Conversation, authority, and the (re)construction of knowledge.* Paper presented at the annual meetings of the American Sociological Association, Washington, DC.

Sasson, T. (1995). *Crime talk: How citizens construct a social problem.* Hawthorne, NY: Aldine.

Seidel, J., Freise, S., & Leonard, D. C. (1995). *The ethnograph v4.0: A user's guide.* Amherst, MA: Qualis Research Associates.

Shively, J. (1992). Cowboys and Indians: Perceptions of Western films among American Indians and anglos. *American Sociological Review, 57,* 724.

Smith, M. W. (1995). Ethics in focus groups: A few concerns. *Qualitative Health Research, 5,* 478-486.

Spradley, J. P. (1979). *The ethnographic interview.* New York: Holt, Rinehart & Winston.

Stewart, D. W., & Shamdasani, P. N. (1990). *Focus groups: Theory and practice.* Newbury Park, CA: Sage.

Strauss, A. L., & Corbin, J. (1990). *Basics of qualitative research.* Newbury Park, CA: Sage.

Sussman, S., Burton, D., Dent, C. W., Stacy, A. W., & Flay, B. R. (1991). Use of focus groups in developing an adolescent tobacco use cessation program: Collective norm effects. *Journal of Applied Social Psychology, 21,* 1772-1782.

Templeton, J. F. (1994). *Focus groups: A guide for marketing and advertising professionals* (Rev. ed.). Burr Ridge, IL: Irwin.

Thompson, J. D., & Demerath, N. N. (1952). Some experiences with the group interview. *Social Forces, 31,* 148-154.

Thorne, B., & Henley, N. (Eds.). (1975). *Language and sex: Difference and dominance.* Rowley, MA: Newbury House.

Thurstone, L. L., & Chave, E. J. (1929). *The measurement of attitude.* Chicago: University of Chicago Press.

Vaughn, S., Schumm, J. S., & Sinagub, J. (1996). *Focus group interviews in education and psychology.* Thousand Oaks, CA: Sage.

Wight, D. (1994). Boys' thoughts and talk about sex in a working class locality of Glasgow. *Sociological Review, 42,* 702-737.

Willis, P. (1977). *Learning to labour: How working class kids get working class jobs.* Westmead, UK: Saxon House.

Yin, R. K. (1994). *Case study research: Design and method* (2nd ed.). Thousand Oaks, CA: Sage.

Zeller, R. A. (1993). Combining qualitative and quantitative techniques to develop culturally sensitive measures. In D. G. Ostrow & R. C. Kessler (Eds.), *Methodological issues in AIDS behavioral research* (pp. 95-116). New York: Plenum.

ABOUT THE AUTHOR

David L. Morgan received his Ph.D. in Sociology from the University of Michigan and did postdoctoral work at Indiana University. He is currently a professor in the Institute on Aging and the Department of Urban Studies and Planning at Portland State University. His research interests center on the ways that people respond to major life changes, which has led him to study retirement communities, nursing homes, widowhood, knowledge about risk factors for heart attacks, caregiving for elderly family members, and, recently, the aging of the Baby Boom generation. When he is not conducting focus groups or writing about them, you may find him hiking in the 5,000 acres of Portland's Forest Park.